CLY*

THE CAREER RESOURCE LIBRARY

Careers
in
Sports Medicine

Barbara Moe

The Rosen Publishing Group, Inc.
NEW YORK

Published in 2002 by The Rosen Publishing Group, Inc.
29 East 21st Street, New York, NY 10010

First Edition

Cover © Aidan/Corbis

Library of Congress Cataloging-in-Publication Data

Moe, Barbara.
Careers in sports medicine / Barbara Moe.
p. cm. — (Career resource library)
Includes bibliographical references and index.
Summary: A discussion of careers in sports medicine and physical therapy, with information on different specializations, training programs, and career preparation.
ISBN 0-8239-3538-8
1. Sports medicine—Vocational guidance—Juvenile literature.
2. Physical therapy—Vocational guidance—Juvenile literature.
[1. Sports medicine—Vocational guidance. 2. Physical therapy—
Vocational guidance. 3. Vocational guidance.] I. Title. II. Series.
RC1210 .M57 2001
617.1'027'023—dc21

2001003490

Manufactured in the United States of America

Contents

Introduction

Sam's recovery from a broken leg led him to a career as an orthopedic surgeon. Kate's love of modern dance led her to a career as an aerobics instructor. Dave hates to exercise. On the rare occasions when he works out, he takes a week to recuperate. But Dave's favorite high school subject was physics; he's heading for a career in biomechanics. These three people, and others in ever-increasing numbers, are choosing careers in sports medicine.

Sports medicine is a subspecialty of medicine, and under its umbrella are other areas of specialization, such as biomechanics, exercise physiology, orthopedics, massage therapy, sports nutrition, and sport psychology. Another way to describe sports medicine is to say it's the science of preventing, diagnosing, and treating athletic injuries. Sports medicine also includes the overlapping discipline of exercise science, which may involve basic research. When we use the term "sports medicine," we may be talking about the clinical as well as the scientific aspects of sports and exercise.

Together, sports medicine and exercise science encompass a range of disciplines. The American College of Sports Medicine and Exercise Science has approximately 18,000 members, which this organization divides into three categories. The category of medicine includes a variety of specialties, such as cardiology (diseases of the heart and circulatory system), podiatry (conditions of the feet), and orthopedics (diseases of the bones and connective tissue). Basic and applied science include such careers as exercise physiology and biomechanics. Education and allied health include athletic trainers, physical therapists, nurses, and physical education teachers.

People who choose careers in sports medicine will work in a variety of settings. For example, as a medical doctor, you may work in a clinic, office, or hospital. As an athletic trainer, you may find yourself in a high school or on a college campus.

Sisters Kelly and Erin Bollig live in Fort Collins, Colorado. Kelly, a junior at Colorado State University, is a premed student who wants to become an orthopedic surgeon. Her older sister is a student athletic trainer for CSU. Both chose a major in health and exercise science. Says Kelly, "Our whole family is involved in sports medicine."

We can categorize sports according to the kind of movements made, the muscles used, and the parts of the body that receive the most stress. For example, running sports, such as football, track, basketball, and soccer, put stress on the knees. Throwing sports, such as baseball or volleyball, put stress on the shoulders and elbows, and sometimes on the fingers. Getting in shape, keeping joints flexible, strengthening muscles—all of these activities help prevent injuries. Many careers in sports medicine are geared toward this type of prevention.

Physical fitness is one of the goals of sports medicine. Physical fitness is a never-ending process that helps people get through their days with energy and sparkle. Physical fitness helps people to think more clearly, may help prevent certain diseases, and improves mood. In the book *Fitness and Sports Medicine,* David C. Nieman distinguishes between skill-related fitness, important in sports, and health-related fitness, which helps people achieve the healthiest body possible given their particular circumstances.

Some careers in sports medicine pay well; others do not. For many people, the main advantage of a sports medicine career is the flexibility (in more ways than one) that their job provides. For example, Kate teaches an aerobics class three times a week and leaves her two-year-old son in the fitness-center nursery. She gets paid for teaching and also keeps herself in shape. For others, job satisfaction is high, even though the salary is not, because they enjoy helping people keep physically fit.

Remember that sports medicine is a subspecialty of medicine, with other subspecialties under its umbrella. Therefore it's important to become a professional in your main career first. For example, become a good doctor, then become a good sports doctor, such as an orthopedic surgeon. Whenever possible in a sports medicine career, find an internship. Besides getting valuable experience in your chosen field, the internship may lead to a job.

Very helpful to anyone considering a career in sports medicine are the following skills: computer knowledge, the ability to speak another language (especially Spanish), and a love of sports. Computers are part of the scene in sports medicine clinics, research laboratories, and fitness centers. And, in our increasingly multiethnic society, speaking another language in addition to English is a definite plus. Finally, because many of your clients will be "jocks," it will be helpful not only to share an enjoyment of sports with your clients but to be able to speak the language of sports.

This book will help you to identify careers in sports medicine that may appeal to you. You will find out what each professional or paraprofessional does, where they work, what qualities people in that field should possess, the education necessary to do the job, and how to get started.

If you are interested in a career in sports medicine, you will find your place.

A Short History of Sports Medicine

1

Depending on your point of view, sports medicine is either very old or rather new. Those who say sports medicine is an old science trace its beginnings as far back as 460 BC to the birth of Hippocrates, often called the father of modern medicine. In ancient Greece during Hippocrates' time, people called sports medicine doctors gymnasts. Hippocrates himself was a gymnast for some of the early Olympic Games.

Others say that the Greek philosopher Aristotle (384–322 BC) started sports medicine with his scientific paper on the walking habits of animals and humans. One of the many things he observed is that a person walking a straight line casts a "zigzag" shadow. This observation may have been the beginning of biomechanics, the study of human movement.

Much later, but still a long time ago, the Italian Leonardo da Vinci (1452–1519) studied and reported on the movement of human beings when faced with such variables as uphill grades and wind resistance. We might call da Vinci the father of modern exercise physiology, the study of bodily changes during exercise.

Three hundred years later, two men from different countries advanced the study of photography along with the science of biomechanics. Etienne Jules Marey, a Frenchman, invented the first force platform, a device to visualize forces between the foot and the floor. Later he studied how a horse runs. Eadweard Muybridge, an American, set up twenty-four different cameras in a row and photographed the motions of a galloping horse. In turn, Marey captured a series of exposures on one photographic plate. Marey also found new ways to measure movement.

By the late 1800s, America had become urban and industrialized. Along with this "progress" came a regression in overall physical fitness. Unlike their agricultural ancestors, later generations of Americans did not get enough exercise at work. Former "hard bodies" became slack. Influential persons of the time noticed this trend and spoke out. Oliver Wendell Holmes, a writer, physician, professor at Harvard Medical School, and Supreme Court justice, urged his fellow Americans to get moving.

As part of their mission, physical educators in schools began to teach young people that exercise could improve the quality of their lives. College prepared physical education teachers and coaches, who tended to emphasize gymnastics instruction based on German and Swedish models. When students rebelled against this emphasis on gymnastics, Dr. Luther Gullick of the YMCA Training School challenged one of his students to come up with a new kind of exercise. As a result, James Naismith invented the game of basketball, a competitive sport that also provided vigorous exercise.

More Modern Times

World War I and World War II forced innovations in sports, medicine, and sports medicine. In 1919, three scientists at Harvard University—Robert Osgood, P. D. Wilson, and Gus Thorndike—established the first sports laboratory in the United States. The focus at this time was on fitness rather than on sports injuries.

As a result of the wars, medical scientists began to try to find ways to work with serious injuries, such as amputations. Later researchers put some of these biomechanical inventions to work in the treatment of athletic injuries. Statistics compiled on those drafted into the armed forces showed a shocking number of young people to be physically unfit. And obesity had become a major health problem. After the war, however, many ex-service people went back to college and joined athletic teams. Women, who had come to the forefront as part of the war effort, contributed to the explosion of interest in sports.

The decade of the 1950s saw many innovations in sports medicine. For one, the focus on fitness (or lack of fitness) turned to young people. In a test of six muscle groups, a large number of United States school children (59 percent) failed, while only 8.7 percent of European children failed. These results led to a White House conference in June 1956 and the subsequent formation of the President's Council on Youth Fitness. Earlier, in 1954, eleven individuals had founded the American College of Sports Medicine, which established for professionals from medicine, physiology, and physical education.

Americans Begin to Exercise

In the 1960s, men and women began to realize that their sedentary habits contributed to heart disease, obesity, and other health problems. After Oregon track coach Bill Bowerman brought the concept of "jogging" to the United States from New Zealand, Americans began to run. They ran in 5K and 10K events and marathons, and participated in iron man competitions.

In 1968, Dr. Kenneth Cooper, an air force physician, published *Aerobics*. This book made popular the concept that exercise should force the body to use oxygen and stimulate the lungs, heart, and blood vessels. As a result of the new revelations about the importance of exercise for cardiovascular health, people began doing more running, walking, biking, and playing competitive sports, such as tennis, basketball, racquetball, and squash. A disciplined study of sport and exercise psychology had begun developing in the late sixties. The North American Society for the Psychology of Sport and Physical Activity (NASPSPA) incorporated in 1967.

In the 1970s, running became symbolic of the exercise movement. For example, in 1972, thousands watched on television as Frank Shorter won the Olympic marathon gold medal. In the same year, James Fixx and others wrote best-selling books about running. Surgeons started using arthroscopic surgery as a diagnostic tool. Today, this surgery to repair tissue damage is the most commonly performed orthopedic surgery in the United States. Spotting an opportunity, businesses began to manufacture exercise equipment like treadmills and stationary bikes. In 1973, Dr. James

Nicholas founded the Institute of Sports Medicine and Athletic Trauma at Lenox Hill Hospital in New York City. Dr. Nicholas had been the team physician for the New York Titans (later the New York Jets) and became interested in treating and preventing sports injuries.

In the 1980s, fitness centers became the rage. The emphasis on cardiorespiratory conditioning continued. The 1990s saw the emergence of a comprehensive approach to physical fitness. In other words, people began to pay attention to both cardiorespiratory conditioning for the heart and lungs and musculoskeletal fitness for strength and endurance. People in the 1990s witnessed competition between the private and public sectors for sports center members. Hospitals and corporations got into the act. At the same time, a trend toward holistic and individualistic training began.

No wonder that with all of this physical activity, the science of sports medicine has grown and continues to grow. Physicians trained in sports medicine repair injuries to ankles, knees, elbows, and shoulders. Exercise physiologists contribute information about training principles, how to avoid dehydration, how the body uses oxygen, and how it builds muscles. Sports nutritionists give advice on weight control and how to eat for exercise and health.

In the future, sports medicine is likely to become more interdisciplinary than it already is. In other words, we can expect to see more overlapping, as well as more competition and cooperation among those in various sports medicine careers.

Physicians and Physical Therapists

2

He's in front of the goal. He spots an opening. A mighty kick. The fans roar. A wrenching pain. Dan falls. His team wins the game, but Dan doesn't go out for pizza. He spends the next couple of hours with ice on his knee waiting to see his family doctor, who tells him to wait for the swelling to go down. His injury might be a type one sprain. The doctor tells Dan to take ibuprofen and gives him a referral to an orthopedic surgeon at a sports medicine clinic.

Four days later, when Dan arrives at the sports medicine clinic, the pain has pretty much disappeared; he can put weight on his leg again. After the exam, the orthopedic surgeon gives Dan the bad news. "You've torn your anterior cruciate ligament. The options are to live with it or to have reconstructive surgery." Dr. Martin explains that without surgery Dan can probably still participate in some sports. Does he like golf? Without surgery, the "cutting" (charging and lurching) sports, such as basketball, football, and soccer, will probably be off limits.

Because Dan hoped to play college soccer, he opted for arthroscopic surgery. His next choice: local or general anesthesia. "I didn't want to be awake," says Dan, "but I knew a general anesthetic was more risky. Still, I didn't want a needle stuck in my spine, so I chose to get knocked out."

Although the surgery went well, the postoperative period was not a piece of cake. "The pain lasted for four or five days," Dan says, "and the swelling didn't disappear for a couple of months. Speaking of pain, it was a pain not to be able to take a shower, not to be able to move around freely, and not to be able to drive my stick-shift car. Do I sound like I'm complaining? I'm not. Before surgery and afterward during rehab, I thought my knee problem was the worst thing that could have happened to me. Now I know my cloud had a silver lining. After about three months, I was able to work out. I'd never done regular workouts with weights before, and now I do it all the time. I think I'm in better shape than I ever was before the surgery."

In the field of sports medicine, physicians and physical therapists work closely together. Rarely is a sports injury treated without some follow-up by a physical therapist. Although there is much overlap, the sports physician is not always an orthopedic surgeon, and an orthopedic surgeon is not always a sports medicine doctor. However, the leader of the sports medicine team is often a physician, specifically an orthopedist. Before we can discuss the subspecialty of sports medicine, we need to find out more about physicians in general.

Generally speaking, physicians are of two major types: doctors of medicine (M.D.s) and doctors of osteopathy (D.O.s). Although they attend different schools, the length of education for M.D.s and D.O.s is about the same. Doctors of osteopathy often work in the prevention of injuries, holistic health, and in disorders of the muscles and bones. D.O.s are licensed to practice the whole spectrum of medicine, but many concentrate on the musculoskeletal system, which may have particular importance to some athletes. Osteopaths sometimes use a technique called osteopathic manipulative treatment, a hands-on approach, to relieve soreness, relax muscles, and restore range of motion.

Approximately one-third of medical doctors and about one-half of osteopathic doctors work as primary-care physicians. Primary-care doctors are on the front lines of medical care; they are often the first physicians to see a patient after an injury and before referral to a specialist, such as an orthopedic surgeon. Primary-care physicians may work in sports medicine with an emphasis on prevention and diagnosis of athletic injuries. However, a large percentage of sports medicine physicians are orthopedic surgeons.

The training for all physicians is long, difficult, and expensive. Most, but not all, applicants to medical school begin with four years of undergraduate education with a scientific emphasis. The premedical curriculum consists of courses in chemistry (organic and inorganic), physics, biology, and mathematics, as well as nonscientific classes in English and possibly another language, social sciences, and the humanities. Much is required of those who apply to medical school. After submitting a transcript of their undergraduate courses, taking the Medical College Admissions Test (MCAT), getting letters of recommendation, and volunteering in hospitals or clinics, they may also have to be interviewed extensively.

In the first two years of medical school, students spend most of their time in laboratories and classrooms, taking such subjects as anatomy and physiology, psychology, biochemistry, microbiology, pathology, and medical ethics. They also study practical subjects such as the interviewing and examination of patients, and they may put their academic courses into action, caring for patients.

John Weaver, a first-year medical student, loves everything about the study of medicine. His father says that beginning in preschool John talked of becoming a doctor and never changed his mind. Because of John's interest in medicine, the Weavers' next-door neighbor, a surgeon, occasionally took John with him when he went on his Saturday morning rounds at the hospital. As a premed student in college, John started a nonprofit corporation to provide medical supplies and money to pediatricians in Africa. The summer after college, he got his EMT (emergency medical technician) certificate in Wyoming and also became IV (intravenous) certified, an extra credential. John also worked as a nurses assistant in a children's hospital. At this point in his education, John isn't sure what medical or surgical specialty he wants to choose. For this high school and college tennis player, a career in sports medicine might have appeal. "He's liked everything he's experienced so far," says his dad, "but whatever he does, I'm sure it will include working with people. He's a real people person."

In the last two years of medical school, students concentrate more on working with patients under the supervision of expert physicians and teachers. They rotate through various medical specialties, such as family practice, obstetrics and gynecology, surgery, internal medicine, pediatrics, and psychiatry. The next step for most physicians is a supervised residency in some medical specialty. The word "residency" no longer means that the doctors-in-training live at the hospital, although many feel as if they do. Hours are long and irregular for residents, who spend much of their time on call.

The years of residency (postgraduate medical education) vary with the specialty and individual choices. Afterward, doctors must pass a licensing exam in their particular state before they are ready to practice medicine. Specialists also need to get certified by the American Board of Medical Specialists (ABMS) in their particular field. The certification for D.O.s is the American Osteopathic Association (AOA).

Although doctors usually have relatively high earnings, their education is costly and most have student loans to repay.

If you are considering a career as a physician with a specialty in sports medicine, ask yourself the following questions: Do I have good grades and am I able to understand scientific material? Do I like working hard and putting in long, irregular hours? Am I willing to be a lifelong student, keeping up with the latest advances in science and medicine? Can I put up with the changes in medical practice, which may involve outside control by health maintenance organizations (HMOs)? Am I emotionally stable?

Doctors from different specialties work in a variety of settings. Sometimes they work in several different settings in a week. These include private offices, group practices, clinics, hospitals, operating rooms, and universities.

Sports Medicine Physicians

Sports medicine doctors work with anyone from the ten-year-old soccer player to the twenty-five-year-old professional basketball player to the forty-year-old tread-mill walker. They do what they can to prevent injuries and treat them when they occur. Sports medicine physicians may specialize in diagnosis and nonsurgical treatment of injuries, or they may do mostly surgery and postoperative care.

Sports medicine doctors may work in a solo practice, or they may work with a group. Even if these doctors do not work with an athletic team, they are "team players." They work with a variety of professionals and paraprofessionals in the health field—from physical therapists to cast-room technicians.

Team doctors make up one subspecialty of sports medicine. Becoming a team physician is a job to which many aspire, but for which few are chosen. Making contacts is the name of the game. Dr. Bridget Dunn is a family practice physician. She got her job as doctor for a women's university's basketball team through an internist friend who was the doctor for the men's university's basketball team. Becoming a team physician, especially for a professional team, is a job that most sports physicians will have to work up to. During medical school and residency, you might volunteer to work with a local team. Or you may want to do a "shadowing" experience with an athletic trainer, coach, or other sports medicine professional, which will give you some sports-related experience. Sometimes, because of their reputations, well-known orthopedic surgeons are picked as team doctors. If you are an assertive person, however, there is no reason you can't apply for a job as a team physician with college or professional teams. Just don't get your hopes up too high. If you do get the job, it may not be a full-time position.

Team physicians have many duties. If you are a person who loves athletics, these jobs may seem like fun. The most important goal of a team physician is to prevent injuries. Helping athletes to stay in shape will involve supervising conditioning programs in cooperation with other team professionals, such as the athletic trainers and coaches. Other aspects of injury prevention include making sure that exercises and drills are safe, helping with the selection of protective equipment, and helping to decide when it is reasonable for an athlete to resume play after an injury.

The team physician will attend games and constantly evaluate an athlete's ability to play. If an injury occurs, others will look to the team doctor to evaluate the situation, give first aid if necessary, and decide what to do next. Team doctors may also conduct team physicals, give advice to athletes about their weight and general health, and counsel them on avoidance of all kinds of substance abuse.

Satisfactions of the job include traveling with the team, getting to know the athletes on all levels, seeing them do their best, and communicating about the players with other professionals and paraprofessionals.

Dr. Kristen Geiger sees patients who have sports injuries in her practice every day. She's a specialist in primary-care sports medicine (the nonsurgical variety). Trained as a pediatrician, she sees mostly young people, ages eighteen and under. What she likes about her job, she says, is that it's a clean thing. Something gets broken, then fixed. "My patients really want to get better; they want to play, to get back in the action." Today Dr. Geiger has just come from her other office across town. In spite of eating lunch in her car, she's a bit late, and patients, some with their arms and legs in casts, are waiting to see her.

Dr. Geiger's first patient of the afternoon is Nicole, a ninth grader who plays volleyball, soccer, basketball, and hockey. Nicole complains that her knees hurt. Earlier today she had X rays of both knees. With the patient lying first on her back, then on her side, then on her front, Dr. Geiger puts Nicole's legs through various ranges of motion. Pressing here and there, she asks, "Does it hurt now? Does your knee feel like it's going to pop? How tight are your hamstrings?"

The tentative diagnosis is complicated. In addition to patellar tendonitis, Dr. Geiger tells Nicole, "You have several things going on at once. That's the bad news. The good news is that a referral to physical therapy and exercises will help." Dr. Geiger shows Nicole her X rays; the bones are fine, and the ligament problems should respond to specific exercises, such as stretching. If the pain persists, Nicole will need to come back in a month.

Dr. Geiger, a soccer player herself, took extra training in orthopedics. "I like this," she said to herself, and her career took off. In addition to her orthopedic talents, she speaks fluent Spanish and is a "sports-o-holic." In her group of physicians, Dr. Geiger has a special place. She is the only physician some of her patients see; she refers others to one of the orthopedic (surgical) specialists in her group. She also works closely with physical therapists, a medical assistant, X-ray technicians, and a cast-room technician.

Orthopedic Surgeons

Only a certain percentage of orthopedic surgeons choose to specialize in sports medicine. The rest see a wide range of patients, from children with cerebral palsy to adults with degenerative bone and joint diseases. Even if they do specialize in sports medicine, they may also practice some general orthopedics.

Orthopedic surgeons developed arthroscopic procedures more than thirty years ago, but at first it was a purely diagnostic and exploratory measure. Using a fiber-optic instrument inserted in the knee, the surgeon could figure out if traditional surgery was needed for tissue damage.

The National Center for Health Statistics reports that knee symptoms are the most common reasons people visit an orthopedist. In sports medicine, the orthopedic surgeon treats various problems connected with the musculoskeletal system, including breaks, sprains, and torn ligaments. They use cutting edge technology, such as microsurgery and metal pieces, to repair damaged bones. In addition to surgery, they prescribe medication, use casts and braces, and make referrals to other professionals, such as physical therapists.

Orthopedic surgeons work in solo practice, in group practice with other orthopedists, or in groups with other subspecialists. Orthopedists often serve as medical directors of sports medicine clinics. They may teach or work as team physicians. Many combinations are possible. Dr. David Greenberg is an orthopedic surgeon who started out in a general orthopedic practice. Then he served as physician for a professional basketball team for five years. After that, he practiced general orthopedics in combination with sports medicine. Finally he opened his own clinic, Sports Conditioning and Orthopedic Rehabilitation, where he worked closely with physical therapists.

If you're considering a career in orthopedic surgery, you should have excellent fine-motor skills. You will work with tools, instruments, screws, and rods. In addition to working with instruments, you will need to be a good communicator—with patients and other members of the sports medicine team. You will also need to be strong, emotionally and physically. The hours are long, as is the training.

In addition to the education received by all physicians, the aspiring orthopedic surgeon will need at least four or five years of postgraduate education and residency. Many orthopedists will take an extra year of fellowship in sports medicine. Later, as practitioners, they go to medical meetings and get continuing education credits from specialized courses.

Sports Cardiologists

One member of the sports medical team has nothing to do with bones and ligaments. The cardiologist deals with a large muscle, the heart, as well as the blood vessels that connect to the heart. Only a small number of cardiologists will work in sports medicine, and most of those who do will serve as consultants. But almost all cardiologists have as one of their goals the prevention of heart disease. Exercise and a healthy diet will help most people avoid an appointment with a cardiologist.

However, there are some cardiologists who devote themselves to evaluating the cardiac status of student athletes. Almost everyone has heard of the apparently healthy college freshman who collapses and dies on the basketball court. Cardiologists can do screening tests to identify potentially serious heart problems. It is not just the young athlete who benefits from such testing. Cardiologists can also evaluate the cardiac status of the fifty-year-old weekend athlete.

The cardiologist uses time-proven tests, such as echocardiography and electrocardiography (EKG), as well as tests using newer technology. Cardiologists also concern themselves with the prevention of heart disease. Their areas of interest include stress reduction, smoking prevention, and cholesterol management.

Cardiology is a subspeciality of internal medicine or pediatrics. In addition to becoming licensed in their states, cardiologists can get certified after a three-year residency in internal medicine or pediatrics, followed by three more years in an accredited cardiology program. Many cardiologists become members of the American College of Cardiology, which indicates a high level of professional practice.

Sports Ophthalmologists

Ophthalmologists are medical doctors who do all kinds of eye care for all ages and types of people, including athletes. They specialize in the treatment and prevention of eye injuries and diseases. In addition to testing vision and prescribing glasses or contact lenses, most also perform eye surgery. In their eye examinations, they sometimes find symptoms of other diseases, such as diabetes, that affect the rest of the body.

Other eye-related careers in sports medicine include optometrists, opticians, ophthalmic technologists, optical laboratory technicians, optometric assistants, and optometric technicians. All of these people may be involved in sports medicine, and their jobs are sometimes grouped together under the heading "sports vision careers."

If you want to be an ophthalmologist, you will first have to become a physician. After medical school, you will need to complete a year of clinical training followed by a three-year residency in ophthalmology. You might even add extra years of training in a subspeciality. The American Board of Ophthalmology certifies candidates who pass the requirements. Ophthalmologists must be recertified every ten years.

Fine-motor skills are important for anyone who does surgery. And, as with other sports medicine specialties, good communication skills and empathy are a must. Athletes with eye problems are worried athletes. Losing a tooth or two is not a huge problem, but the loss of vision is a scary prospect.

The Rehabilitation Team

Anyone who has had surgery for a sports injury will tell you that "rehab" is a critical part of sports medicine. Physical therapists (PTs) and occupational therapists (OTs), all members of the rehabilitation team, work with people who have problems with various kinds of movements. Physical therapists work with those who are recovering or learning to live with injuries and diseases of muscles, joints, bones, and nerves. Occupational therapists are more likely to help people improve their fine-motor skills, such as finger movements. Although OTs are valuable members of the rehabilitation team, they are not as commonly used in sports medicine as PTs.

Physical therapists deal with musculoskeletal problems—problems of the muscles, bones, and ligaments. A physician who specializes in sports therapy might see patients when they are starting to get mobility back after surgery or injury. Sometimes, people refer to physical therapist physicians as rehab doctors.

These physicians help people regain optimum mobility after injuries or diseases, or from conditions they are born with. They work with other doctors and various other rehabilitation specialists, including nurses, prosthetists, and orthotists. They may work in a sports medicine clinic, hospital, rehabilitation center, medical center, or research center.

A survey of 200 randomly selected sports medicine centers showed that almost every center employed a physical therapist. In fact, at 70 percent of these centers, a physical therapist served as clinical director. In a sports medicine setting, physical therapists may supervise physical therapy assistants and aides. They may also work with nurses, occupational therapists and aides, podiatrists, and exercise physiologists.

Physical therapists need to be able to examine and evaluate clients by taking careful histories and using specific tests and measurements. They check balance and coordination, muscle strength, range of motion, and posture. They need to be able to figure out the best plan of treatment and estimate how long the treatment will take. After they make a plan of treatment, they have to be able to modify the plan as special circumstances develop. In doing their work, physical therapists make use of heat and cold, water, sound, electricity, traction, deep-tissue massage, and passive motion machines.

Many physical therapists who specialize in sports medicine work in hospitals, but even more work in clinics, community and sports centers, industrial centers, universities, research institutions, and private homes. Some physical therapists own and operate their own private practices.

When Dan stayed overnight in the hospital after his knee surgery, a physical therapist came to his room to show him how to use his crutches. Several weeks later, Dan went to rehab and worked with a different physical therapist. "It basically looked like a gym," says Dan, "with tons of equipment—tables, machines, and weights." Dan went to rehab twice a week for about seven weeks. "I tried to get the same physical therapist each time because I liked her. With her supervision, I worked against my body weight doing things like balancing on one foot, dips (standing on the repaired leg and squatting), walking on stairs, riding the stationary bike, and pulling on a bungee cord attached to the wall."

Do you enjoy studying sciences such as anatomy, physiology, chemistry, physics, and psychology? Do you like working with people? Do you have good grades? Are you physically strong? Physical therapists often need to work with heavy pieces of equipment. They also may have to help their patients stand and move.

If you are interested in a career as a physical therapist, it is best to apply to a school of physical therapy after you have already gotten a master's degree. You should also plan to do some volunteer work in the field.

Not only will you make yourself more desirable to the school, but in the process you will learn something about the profession. All levels of the program include clinical experiences. Those getting a doctorate in physical therapy will need to have an internship. As with most other careers in sports medicine, cultural diversity is valued. The American Physical Therapy Association has made a commitment to help recruit minority students to the program.

After graduation from an accredited program, you will have to pass a licensing exam, a national test administered by your state. Other requirements for practicing physical therapy vary from state to state. For information on licensing, you can call the Federation of State Boards of Physical Therapy at (800) 200-3031, or visit their Web site at http://www.fsbpt.org.

Exercise and Fitness Specialists

3

You'll find exercise and fitness specialists in the health club, on the athletic field, in the gym, and in the laboratory. Careers in this field include exercise physiologists, aerobics instructors and personal trainers, athletic trainers, and strength and conditioning coaches. Fitness equipment designers and salespeople would also fit into this category, but as one exercise physiologist put it, "How many treadmills can you sell?"

Exercise physiology is the discipline that deals with the functioning of the human body and how it responds to exercise. The study of exercise physiology can lead to careers in research, or it can apply to clinical sports medicine. Those who apply their knowledge of exercise physiology to clinical sports medicine will most likely work with people to help them increase or better tolerate exercise. Exercise physiologists use all kinds of modern technology, including videotapes, computers, and slow-motion photography, to achieve their goals.

So what exactly do exercise physiologists do? The answer is not a simple one because you will find that exercise physiology is the basis for many different careers in sports medicine. Exercise physiologists may become instructors and directors of fitness centers, health clubs, spas, or resorts. They may become strength and conditioning coaches at colleges and universities, exercise specialists in cardiac rehabilitation centers, or researchers in chemical and physical changes that take place in the heart, lungs, and muscles. They might become personal trainers or instructors, or professors at the college level.

People with degrees in exercise physiology are busy defining their roles and finding new ones. Exercise physiologists are pushing the frontiers of sports medicine. A degree in exercise physiology may be your ticket to a job, or it may be the first step toward a graduate degree. Some people get an undergraduate degree in a related field, such as physical education, and then follow it up with a master's degree in exercise physiology. Michelle Haugh is aiming for her master's degree in health and exercise science. Because she got her bachelor's degree in psychology, she has to "re-do" her B.A. and is now taking prerequisites for the master's program. Michelle, who has worked as a personal trainer for five years, got certified through the American Council on Exercise. Her eventual goal is to get a Ph.D. and to become a sports psychologist. If you think you would like a career in sports medicine but aren't sure of your area of specialization, a degree in exercise physiology might be a wise choice for you.

In the four-year undergraduate program, students are likely to take such subjects as chemistry (organic and inorganic), physics, anatomy, physiology, kinesiology, and cell physiology. An interest in science is a must. Other desirable qualities include strong communication skills and the ability to work with all kinds of people.

Exercise physiologists can get certified through a number of organizations, including the National Strength and Conditioning Association, the American College of Sports Medicine, the American Society of Exercise Physiologists, and the American Council on Exercise.

Aerobics Instructors and Personal Trainers

Aerobics instructors and personal trainers lead exercises for individuals and groups in fitness centers, health clubs, gyms, and community centers. Personal trainers sometimes work one-on-one in clients' homes. Wherever they work, they first evaluate the person's strength, flexibility, and abilities. They often design a personal fitness plan for that individual. They may meet with their clients once a week or more often to keep them on track, to demonstrate new machines and exercises, to check if they're correctly using the equipment, and to give advice and encouragement. Some personal trainers are self-employed.

Aerobics instructors tend to lead group activities that contribute to aerobic fitness. One small health club lists the names of twenty-seven instructors (mostly women), and the following aerobics and conditioning classes: high- and low-impact aerobics, muscle conditioning, water aerobics, total body conditioning, cross-training workout, extreme total conditioning, cardio-kickboxing, yoga, and tae kwon do, to mention just a few.

As mentioned earlier, one of the advantages of a career as an aerobics instructor or personal trainer is flexibility. However, what some people consider an advantage, others consider a disadvantage; some people want a regular 9 AM to 5 PM schedule. Usually the pay is not high; the instructor or trainer may receive an hourly wage. Do you have boundless energy? Do you love working out? Are you able to motivate others to work out? Do you get along well with all types of people? Then you might consider one of these careers as a part-time job.

Some aerobics instructors and personal trainers have college degrees, such as a degree in physical education or exercise physiology. Some do not have college degrees or have degrees in other majors. Some are certified and some are not. Some are on salary at health clubs.

Neil Bogan currently works full-time at a health club. He's a personal trainer with several certifications to his credit. Besides that, he's friendly and personable. The clients who work with him feel as if they're in capable hands. Neil is a certified strength and conditioning specialist, a certified athletic trainer, and a certified physical therapist. He has an undergraduate degree in kinesiology and a master's degree in physical therapy.

Athletic Trainers

Erin Ryan got her start as an athletic trainer in high school. "I took a class at the Career Education Center and after that I got a scholarship at Regis University, where I worked as a trainer for two years for the girls' soccer team. I wrapped ankles, iced knees, and got to go on all the trips. It was great fun."

Tom Healian's career goes back further than Erin's. Tom graduated from high school in 1948 and went to college at Miami University in Oxford, Ohio. He'd always been interested in sports. One of his high school teachers told him to go into the training room at a local college and introduce himself. Tom's thirty-two-year career as an athletic trainer began the day he walked into the training room and asked, "Do you need some help?" Back then he worked for thirty-five cents an hour, seven days a week, for four years. "I met a lot of coaches," Tom says, "and every job I ever got came about from someone I knew."

Tom progressed, spent two years as an assistant trainer at two different colleges, then became head trainer at Northwestern University, where he worked for eight years with legendary coach Ara Parsegian. Later, he took another head training job at Indiana University. From there Tom moved to Boston and spent twelve years as trainer with the New England Patriots professional football team. Although the job of a trainer with a professional team sounds glamorous, Tom enjoyed his college jobs even more. He liked the camaraderie of being a university faculty member, and he liked getting to know the young athletes in various sports. Some difficulties of the job included the long hours during football and basketball seasons, and being away from home on many major holidays.

Athletic trainers are also called certified athletic trainers, sports trainers, certified sports medicine trainers, or certified sports medicine therapists. No matter what people call them, athletic trainers are vital members of the sports medicine team. They work in cooperation with team physicians and coaches in preventing injuries, treating injuries when they occur, and helping injured athletes with rehabilitation services. They are front-line professionals.

The duties of athletic trainers do not end after the game. Other responsibilities may include administrative duties, such as developing a budget or supervising a student trainer program. Trainers also have to be able to communicate with physicians, members of the coaching staff, relatives and friends of injured athletes, and the athletes themselves. They have to organize athletes' physicals and keep medical files, order medical supplies and monitor their use, analyze athletes' readiness to participate, and help to decide when an injured athlete is ready to return to the game. They may also select and recommend specific exercises for specific athletes, check fields or playing areas for potential hazards, select protective equipment, and use emergency procedures for serious injuries in order to stabilize athletes after a concussion or fracture.

Athletic trainers work in high schools, community colleges, and universities. Some work for professional sports teams. Others work in businesses, such as health clubs or sports medicine clinics. Most trainers love sports and have usually been participants themselves. If you are considering a career as a trainer, you should be able to keep a cool head in emergencies, stay calm at the sight of blood or broken bones, and enjoy science courses. A trainer needs to have a great deal of energy and should be organized in order to juggle the responsibilities that go with the job. A willingness to help others and an ability to get along with all kinds of people are musts.

If you're in high school and think you would like a career as an athletic trainer, take as many science classes as you can handle, such as anatomy and physiology, and get certified in CPR and first aid. Participate in as many sports as you can, and see if you can volunteer to work with a trainer to get on-the-job experience. Continue all of this in college.

Athletic trainers need to have a bachelor's degree in an accredited program, with possible concentrations in kinesiology, physical exercise science, athletic training, and health education. Courses will include anatomy, physiology, nutrition, athletic training, and psychology. Students will serve internships with sports teams or in health clubs, and get other clinical experience. You might want to consider getting a teaching credential, which will make you even more valuable in a high school setting.

As you go through your education, you will learn all of the requirements for certification and find out various ways you can get certification, which is required in more than half of the fifty states. For example, to get certified by the National Athletic Trainers' Association, you will need a bachelor's degree from an accredited program and you will have to pass a certifying examination.

Be ready to keep your skills current by taking continuing education courses. And consider joining a professional organization, such as the National Athletic Trainers' Association. Although you may think of athletic trainers as mostly men, 40 percent of the members of the NATA are women.

Strength and Conditioning Coaches

Strength training is the use of progressive resistance to increase a person's ability to exert or resist force. This ability is important for all athletes who use body weights, free weights, and machines to get results. The benefits of weight training include improved endurance, muscle strength, and performance. On a simple level, the strength and conditioning coach is in charge of weight-lifting activities for college and professional athletic teams. But today, with many athletes and even nonathletes recognizing the benefits of weight training, this field is expanding. The weight-training specialist helps rehabilitate athletes after injuries and also tries to prevent injuries.

In a university program, health club, or corporate fitness center, the strength and conditioning coach establishes and supervises physical conditioning programs and also supervises weight-room activities. The weight-training specialist may also develop weight-training activities specific to a certain sport. For example, the muscle strength and endurance needed by a golfer is different from that needed by a soccer player.

A four-year college degree is important for a strength and conditioning coach, as is certification. The National Strength and Conditioning Association (NSCA) is the professional organization that certifies people in this sports medicine specialty. These credentials include the Certified Strength and Conditioning Specialist (CSCS) and the NSCA Certified Personal Trainer (NSCA-CPT). Members of this organization include not only strength and conditioning coaches but also athletic trainers, personal trainers, exercise physiologists, physical therapists, fitness directors, aerobics instructors, researchers, sports coaches, and students interested in any of these fields.

Related Sports Medicine Careers

4

Related sports medicine careers require at least three or four years of college, and some require more. Most of these related careers require certification, as well as clinical experience. A person who gets a job in one of these areas may work full-time in the sports medicine specialty, but most people will also need to do some additional general work in their field before specializing.

Biomedical Engineer

Biomedical engineers are also called biomechanists. Biomechanics is the science that investigates the effects of internal and external forces on human bodies at rest and in motion. Through this discipline, scientists learn about the intricacies of movement and how these movements affect an athlete's performance and sometimes cause injuries. Biomedical engineers in sports medicine use their skills to devise or improve instruments and substances to help athletes. Using basic principles of biology and physics, they serve as a connection between the world of medicine and the world of engineering.

The continuous passive motion device (CPM) was introduced in the early 1970s by Dr. Robert B. Salter of the Hospital for Sick Children in Toronto, Canada. It passively moves a patient's joints through a predetermined range of motion. These passive devices are used not only with knees but also with hips, ankles, shoulders, elbows, wrists, and hands. The CPM is a motorized instrument with two parts—a carriage that supports the part of the body surrounding the immobilized joint, and a controller that is programmed for ranges of motion and speed. Biomedical engineers design devices such as the CPM to help athletes return to action as soon as possible after injuries or surgery. In this way, engineers enter the field of sports medicine.

Biomedical engineers work in research centers performing tests on animals and humans, or they may work in marketing and sales or in shops that build models of new machines. Biomedical engineers also work in hospitals, in laboratories, and for large corporations. Those in sales and marketing may spend much of their time on the road.

If you are considering a career in biomedical engineering, you should have a strong math and science background. Take as many science courses as you can, in addition to math courses. You should have good oral and written communication skills because you will need to exchange ideas with professionals in other disciplines, especially people in medicine and other areas of engineering, such as electrical and chemical engineering.

Biomedical engineers are inventors and problem solvers who love a challenge.

Most biomedical engineers have a bachelor's degree and an advanced degree, such as a master's or doctorate. In the first two years of undergraduate school, students take theoretical sciences; in the second two years, they branch out to apply this knowledge. While working on advanced degrees, students may get involved in research projects under faculty supervision at the university, or with a private corporation. As with any career in sports medicine, an internship is a plus, as are certification and membership in professional organizations like the Biomedical Engineering Society.

Sports Dentistry

Mike Dunn is a team dentist. However, at one time he considered a career as an accountant. What made him hesitate was that his accountant father, after many years with a big firm, had gotten laid off and then struggled to find work. Encouraged by his dad to become a doctor or a dentist, Mike liked the idea of being his own boss. His uncle, an oral surgeon, became his role model.

How did he become a sports dentist? Actually, Mike says it was his wife's doing. Years ago, Peggy played tennis with a woman whose husband was general manager of the Denver Nuggets. The team dentist at the time didn't like basketball. Mike and Peggy did. Both had played basketball in high school and loved the game. Twenty-five years later, Mike and Peggy are still attending Nuggets games. According to Mike, it's a league rule that a dentist be present at every game. In fact, a group of ophthalmologists rotates the responsibility for emergency eye care at the games, an orthopedic surgeon attends every game, and an internist is there 80 percent of the time.

Mike says that in addition to the fun of watching the games, he has gotten many referrals for his practice. He enjoys interacting with the players and coaches. He and Peggy have made many longtime friends. Does he have any advice for those considering a career in sports dentistry? "Show an interest," says Mike, "and establish contacts." He adds that Peggy looks at it this way: "It's all a matter of timing and contacts."

Dentists work in one area of the body: the mouth. Even though their treatment site is small, the job of a dentist is surprisingly varied. Dentists find and fill cavities, of course, but they also pull teeth, fit people with artificial teeth, build bridges, perform root canals, treat gum disease, give anesthesia, and prescribe medication. Sometimes they also clean teeth, order supplies, and take X rays. In addition, they are usually the ones who make sure that the dental equipment is functioning.

Because most dentists work in private practices, they also have to run a small business. They hire and supervise other employees, such as dental hygienists, dental assistants, dental laboratory technicians, receptionists, and sometimes an office manager. The dentist or others under his or her supervision have to cope with different health insurance companies and must also comply with governmental regulations. They work with many different pieces of equipment, such as drills, X-ray machines, probes, forceps, mirrors, scalpels, and brushes. Prevention of dental problems is another important job for dentists and their employees. They teach their patients about dental hygiene, including proper brushing and flossing techniques, as well as proper eating habits.

Dentistry has many subspecialties. Some specialists are orthodontists, who realign teeth with braces; endodontists, who treat infected tissue inside the teeth; pedodontists, who treat children's teeth; periodontists, who deal with gum problems; and prosthodontists, who make false teeth. And, of course, there are sports medicine dentists. Most sports dentists would have a hard time surviving if sports dentistry were all they did. Most, like Mike Dunn, have a busy private practice as well. Some dentists are consultants to athletic teams and receive a salary, while others work as volunteers.

A sports dentist who works with a particular team will undoubtedly be involved with mouth protectors. In addition, the team dentist may have to decide what to do in a dental emergency, at least until the athlete can see his or her regular dentist. A team dentist should also perform preventative activities, such as teaching the players and athletes about good dental health.

Becoming a dentist requires hard work. If you're interested in this profession, put some emphasis on science courses in high school. Do you have good manual dexterity? If you have shaky hands, dentistry is probably not for you. You should have a gentle touch and a reassuring manner. Some people are terrified of dentists and dental work. You should also be a good communicator. Someone has to do the talking when the patient's mouth is full of dental equipment!

Most dental schools require a bachelor's degree with course concentration in the sciences. If you want to apply to dental school, which takes four additional years after college, you will need to take the Dental Admissions Test (DAT) and get a good score. You will need a high grade-point average, and you should expect interviews.

As in medical school, the first two years of dental school are mostly academic, with a heavy emphasis on sciences like anatomy and physiology, microbiology, and biochemistry. In the second two years, the emphasis shifts to clinical practice in dental clinics and offices under the supervision of licensed dentists. When you graduate from an accredited dental school, your degree is most likely to be Doctor of Dental Surgery (D.D.S.). Some graduates get a Doctor of Dental Medicine (D.M.D.) degree. You will also need to pass a written and practical test to get your dental license. Specialists will need between two and five additional years of post-graduate education.

Sports Psychologists

Do you like to get inside other people's heads and try to figure out what makes them tick? Then you may want to choose a career in psychology. Add to that a love of sports and you're on your way. Chances are that you will have to supplement your income at least for a while; a full-time career in sports psychology will take some working up to.

Sports psychologists work with the inner person and the "inner game," helping athletes to overcome problems that decrease their performance. These problems may be related to participation in the game itself and may be caused by nervousness, anxiety, or low self-esteem. On the other hand, athletes may have worries about other matters that affect their performance, such as problems with a spouse or kids, financial difficulties, or substance abuse.

As a discipline, sports psychology is concerned with two major factors: how can athletes use the scientific principles of psychology to enhance their athletic performance and how does physical activity contribute to a person's mental health, physical health, and overall sense of well-being.

Where sports psychologists work is directly related to with whom they work. If you're a sports psychologist working with a team, you may find yourself on a football field or in a gym. If you're doing research, you may work in an exercise performance lab. If you're counseling an individual athlete, you may work in a quiet office. Sports psychologists sometimes have their own private practices, or they may join a group practice. They may receive a salary from a school district, college, university, or sports team.

Sports psychologists work with individual athletes, both amateur and professional, or with teams as a group to promote a winning attitude. Sports psychologists can also be helpful when, in spite of everyone's best efforts on the field, things do not go as well as expected.

Just as physicians must become doctors before they become sports doctors, sports psychologists must first become psychologists. Most people who work as psychologists have a doctoral degree in psychology. If you are interested in a career as a psychologist, you might get your undergraduate degree in psychology, although a major in psychology is not absolutely necessary. Students with degrees in other fields are often able to get into a master's program in psychology. Be sure to take psychology classes along with courses in social sciences, physical sciences, mathematics, statistics, and a language such as French or German. Get good grades; getting into a psychology graduate school program will be very competitive.

A typical master's program takes two years of postgraduate work. Usually, you will also have some supervised clinical practice in a school or health-care setting. After you get your master's degree, you will need between two and five more years to get a doctorate. You can choose one of two routes to achieve this goal. A Ph.D. usually requires the student to write a dissertation and is more oriented to research. The other route, a Psy.D. degree, is more oriented toward clinical practice and may not require a dissertation. An internship will be important in all programs.

There are several ways to become a sports psychologist. One way is to get a doctorate in sports sciences and get extra training in counseling and psychology. Another way is to get a doctorate in psychology and then take extra courses in sports sciences. If you are interested in sports psychology as a career and want to know about requirements for licensing in your state, contact the American Psychological Association (APA), or visit their Web site at http://www.apa.org.

Sports Nutritionists and Dieticians

Jackie Berning is the sports nutritionist/dietician for a professional baseball team, a professional football team, and a university football team. She is also a college professor and the current spokesperson for the American Dietetic Association. "She's very busy," says a friend, also a dietician. "A lot of people call themselves sport nutritionists, but they really aren't. She is!"

The terms "dietician" and "nutritionist" are sometimes used interchangeably. Both plan food and nutrition programs. They promote healthy eating habits and suggest dietary modifications for those who need them. Some people call dieticians and nutritionists "food coaches."

People who call themselves sports dieticians are likely to be registered dieticians (RD). They have finished academic requirements, have had practical experience, and have passed a certification exam. Sports nutritionists may, of course, be dieticians, but they may also have come from such backgrounds as medicine, nursing, athletic training, or physical therapy. There are no specific requirements for calling yourself a nutritionist, but most nutritionists have had at least two years of college-level training in nutrition or have served an internship.

Sports dieticians and nutritionists are most likely to serve as consultants to one or more sports teams, and they may also have a private practice. Or they may work under contract with a health organization or a physical fitness facility. In their work they give advice on dietary matters thought to affect athletic performance, such as weight loss or weight gain, the importance of adequate hydration, the dangers of skipping meals, reduction of cholesterol levels, and how to evaluate claims for nutritional supplements. Some nutritionists work at colleges and universities, advising members of sports teams or doing basic research. Others work for corporations or cardiac rehabilitation centers.

If you are a high school student thinking of becoming a dietician or nutritionist, be sure to take as many science and health-related courses as possible. Depending on your college, you may be able to find a sports nutrition major. You'll certainly have to take college-level science courses, along with pertinent courses in business, computers, nutrition, and exercise science. As a sports nutritionist, you will have an interest in healthy foods and will need to communicate that information to coaches, athletic trainers, and the players themselves. You will need to have good writing and speaking skills.

Not all states require licenses for dieticians and nutritionists, but getting as many credentials as possible is always a good idea. To be able to use the initials "RD" after your name, you must have a bachelor's degree from an accredited university, take courses approved by a branch of the American Dietetic Association, and complete a supervised clinical program. After that, you will have to pass an examination given by the Commission on Dietetic Registration. If you want to do research or teach at the college level, you will need a graduate degree.

If you're interested in working with a sports team, get to know coaches and players. You may want to work for a while as a volunteer. Read sports nutrition literature and plan to take continuing education courses.

Orthotists and Prosthetists

Orthotics and prosthetics are two related disciplines with separate goals. Orthotists design, construct, and fit braces and other supports to correct parts of the body weakened by injury or disease. Orthotists work in connection with other specialists, such as the patient's primary physician, orthopedists, podiatrists, biomechanists, and physical therapists.

In a general practice, the orthotist will work with all ages and conditions, from an elderly man who has had a stroke to a little boy with muscular dystrophy. In the practice of sports orthotics, the orthotist will work with athletes. Many orthotists will combine a general practice with some sports medicine.

John is an avid racquetball player who developed plantar fascitis in both feet. His feet ached when he walked, and he had to give up his daily games of racquetball. He couldn't wait to get his orthoses (foot supports), which helped the pain at least when he walked. He's still not back on the racquetball court.

The work of an orthotist is varied. A physician may ask the orthotist for a specific kind of brace, or the referring doctor may send the patient with a prescription stating the diagnosis and asking the orthotist to design the appropriate support. The orthotist will meet with the patient, do muscle testing, check the person's range of motion, take measurements, and consult with the referring physician about the best type of support for the condition.

Orthotists work with precision tools. They need to have good manual dexterity. Orthotists use drills, saws, glue, velcro, wood, plastic, fiberglass, aluminum, and other materials. Orthotists also make drawings, casts, and braces. The aspiring orthotist should like the challenge of solving problems for a client. Orthotists also work with computers to make "blueprints" of the needed orthoses, taking into consideration a patient's height, weight, and level of physical activity.

Prosthetists work with physicians and other professionals to make devices to help those who have lost a limb or part of a limb. Prostheses help people to carry on with activities of daily living and sometimes allow them to participate in athletics.

Prosthetists make prostheses (or, if just one, a prosthesis) for those who have lost a hand, arm, leg, or a foot because of accidents or birth disabilities. Referring physicians usually write a prescription, and the prosthetist determines the best type of device to help the patient. Prosthetists measure the remaining limb and work with a technician to make a cast. During fitting sessions, prosthetists make sure the prosthesis fits comfortably, without pressure points that cause pain. Prosthetists may also work with myoelectric technology, which uses motorized components to allow the prosthesis to move.

Because of the closeness of orthotics and prosthetics, some people combine the two careers. Work settings include private practices, sports medicine clinics, hospitals, research facilities, and universities. If you are interested in being an orthotist or a prosthetist, or in combining these two careers, you will need to develop strong communication skills. It will be important to be able to talk with various members of the sports medicine team, as well as with your patients. A combination of the two careers will provide variety; you will not get bored.

Either career or both careers together require knowledge of sciences, especially anatomy, biology, physics, and chemistry. Also helpful will be computer classes and shop classes. Of course, any classes that teach communication skills, such as English and speech, will also be important high school courses. In college, the same type of course work will also be important. If you are sure of your career choice, you can get a bachelor of science degree in orthotics and prosthetics from a school accredited by the National Commission on Orthotic and Prosthetic Education (NCOPE). If you're not sure, you can get a bachelor of science or bachelor of arts degree with another major and then, after college, complete a one-year certificate program. Most aspiring orthotists and prosthetists also add a one-year residency in an NCOPE program. Practical experience, before the residency, possibly as a technician, is valuable.

Licensing requirements vary from state to state. The American Board for Certification in Orthotics and Prosthetics, Inc., certifies orthotists and prosthetists. While certification is not mandatory, it is recommended. You may then put one of three sets of initials after your name: CO stands for certified orthotist, CP signifies certified prosthetist, and CPO means certified prosthetist-orthotist.

Registered Nurses

The term "registered nurse" covers a variety of subspecialties within this profession; sports medicine is one of these specialties. A nurse who specializes in sports medicine will probably have worked in the office of an orthopedist, in a sports medicine clinic, or with an orthopedic unit in a hospital. In a hospital setting, the nurse may have to work rotating shifts, including nights, weekends, and holidays. Registered nurses work under the supervision of physicians but sometimes supervise other personnel, such as licensed practical nurses, medical assistants, and nurses' aides. Registered nurses interact with other members of the sports medicine team, including physical therapists, nutritionists, orthotists, and prosthetists.

Registered nurses (RNs) carry out the treatments ordered by doctors and also make treatment plans of their own. They assist physicians with procedures and perform procedures of their own. Some nurses function as case managers, coordinating various aspects of patient care. When they provide direct care, nurses take vital signs (pulse, body temperature, and rate of respiration), record symptoms and reactions, administer medications, give baths and massages, and get patients out of bed and moving around. Most nurses wish for more time to talk with patients and their families. Nurses also work in the prevention of disease and the promotion of health.

Do you think you might like to become a nurse? Guys are eligible, too, you know. Nurses are usually compassionate, empathetic types with good people skills. Being able to handle emergencies is desirable, but not all nurses work in emergency rooms. Nurses need to be able to follow doctors' orders, but they should also be able to see the big picture and make their own observations.

Courses to take in high school include sciences, such as biology, chemistry, and psychology; communication courses, such as English and speech; a second language; and computer courses. If possible, volunteer as a candy striper in a hospital or work as a nurses' aide. In college or nursing school, nursing students take science courses, such as anatomy and physiology, nutrition, chemistry, and microbiology, in addition to clinical practice classes. The education goes beyond the classroom into hospitals and clinics, where nursing students receive supervised experience in the various specialties—medical, surgical, obstetric, psychiatric, and public health.

To become a registered nurse, a person has to graduate from a nursing program and pass a national licensing exam. If you are interested in a career in nursing, you will take one of three routes. You can attend a community or junior college and receive an associate's degree in nursing (A.D.N.). You can go to a university and, after a four- or five-year program, get a bachelor of science degree in nursing (B.S.N.). The third route is the hospital-based or diploma program, which is two or three years long. These programs are much less common today than they were several decades ago, before corporations took over so many of the church-sponsored hospitals.

Graduates of all of these programs who become licensed qualify for positions as staff nurses, but some institutions prefer those with bachelor's degrees. The B.S.N. will usually lead to faster advancement in the profession. Some graduates of community college or diploma programs take advantage of tuition reimbursements and go for their B.S.N.

Physician Assistants

Some people have never heard of physician assistants, or if they have, they get them mixed up with medical assistants. Like medical assistants and registered nurses, physician assistants work under the supervision of a doctor, but PAs do some of the same jobs as physicians. Dr. Kristen Geiger says that the physician assistant in her office duplicates many of her duties.

As members of the sports medicine team, physician assistants may treat uncomplicated fractures with casting and splinting, and other sports injuries with suturing. They also take patients' histories, examine patients, and order laboratory tests and X rays. They make notes in patients' charts, and counsel and teach patients. In all but a few states, physician assistants can write prescriptions for medication. They may supervise technicians, such as X-ray technicians or those in the cast room. They may also be in charge of ordering medical supplies.

Although physician assistants work under the supervision of physicians, this supervision may be less intense in rural areas. Modern technology facilitates communication between the PA and the supervising doctor. Physician assistants are especially sought after in places where the supply of physicians is limited. In fact, the specialty was started in the 1960s as a response to a shortage of doctors in some areas of the country. PAs usually work in an office but may assist in surgery. Some have more than one job. Their schedules may be tied to the schedule of the physician who supervises them. They may also have to work weekends and evenings and be on call.

If you are considering a career as a physician assistant, you should enjoy communicating with people and not mind working under the direction of someone else. You should, however, also be able to make your own decisions. You should be ready to spend the rest of your working life keeping up with advances in medicine and be willing to teach patients and coworkers. Courses to take in high school include the sciences, such as chemistry, physics, and biology, as well as English, speech, and a second language. Volunteer experience in a hospital or clinic will be useful. Competition for admission into PA programs is fierce, and preference may be given to those who have worked in other medical fields, such as nursing or physical therapy. Many applicants to PA schools have bachelor's or even master's degrees.

Some people have called physician assistants "junior doctors," and their training a miniature medical school. For admission into most PA programs, at least two years of college is required. The PA program itself usually takes two additional years. Programs are often associated with medical schools. The curriculum includes science courses, such as anatomy and physiology, microbiology, pharmacology, and nutrition, as well as clinical courses and supervised clinical practice in various medical specialties.

Physician assistants have to pass the Physician Assistants National Certifying Examination administered by the National Commission on Certification of Physician Assistants (NCCPA). Those who pass the exam can use the initials PA-C, meaning Physician Assistant-Certified. To remain certified, physician assistants have to take 100 hours of continuing medical education every two years. Every six years, they have to pass a recertification exam.

Sports Optometrists

Optometrists are not ophthalmologists, but they do some of the same things. Optometrists provide primary eye care, which involves examining eyes, diagnosing and treating eye diseases, and prescribing glasses, contact lenses, and medications. Optometrists often work in cooperation with ophthalmologists. Optometrists sometimes practice vision therapy, and in sports medicine they may perform vision training for specific sports. Some athletes who have had this type of training say it has improved their game.

Many optometrists have a solo practice and have to handle the business aspects of their work, such as hiring and firing, keeping patient records, billing patients, and ordering supplies. Some work in partnerships or group practices. Others work in health maintenance organizations or in retail stores.

Optometrists need to have at least three years of college before they will be admitted to a four-year college of optometry. To get in, applicants have to take the Optometry Admissions Test. All fifty states and the District of Columbia require licensing. Applicants have to have a Doctor of Optometry degree from an accredited school and must pass a written and clinical state board examination.

Holistic Sports Medicine Careers

5

The potential for holistic sports medicine careers is almost endless. Holistic implies the use of therapies outside the mainstream of medicine. Practitioners of holistic medicine say they look at the whole person, not just at a body part. Some people, including athletes, turn to nontraditional therapies when traditional medical practices fail. Other people start with nontraditional therapies and then turn back to traditional medicine. Sometimes people utilize both kinds of treatment at the same time.

Athletes may look to holistic physicians in addition to or instead of traditional doctors. Holistic physicians have to have the same credentials as conventional doctors. Holistic doctors may refer patients to traditional specialists, but they may also prescribe natural remedies. According to the *Encyclopedia of Careers and Vocational Guidance,* nearly one-third of traditional schools of medicine currently include courses in alternative treatments in their programs.

Acupuncturists

Acupuncturists insert needles in various locations of the body to relieve pain and treat addictions, such as smoking and drinking. Before acupuncture there was acupressure, used by the Chinese more than 5,000 years ago. Acupressure and acupuncture are said to stimulate the flow of vital energy, called chi, moving along fourteen pathways, or meridians. Practitioners believe that their therapies can unblock or restore the balance of energy in the body. Acupressure uses thumb and finger pressure instead of needles.

Acupuncturists take patients' histories, do physical examinations, and make observations about their patients. They try to figure out the reason for the energy imbalance as a way of picking the appropriate needle and its insertion site. Acupuncturists may also suggest herbal remedies to their patients. Some acupuncturists add this role to their ongoing careers in general medicine or sports medicine. For example, a chiropractor may take training to become an acupuncturist.

Acupuncturists who have a private practice will also need to have business management skills. If you are interested in becoming an acupuncturist, you should take science, math, and computer courses in high school, and also learn what you can about nontraditional healing methods. For example, community schools and exercise centers often offer classes in yoga and tai chi. As a sports acupuncturist, you need to have empathy for people who are in pain. Self-esteem and confidence are also important qualities for an acupuncturist. Because many people in this country do not believe in nontraditional therapies, you will need to have a thick skin.

Educational requirements vary. The United States has about fifty schools of acupuncture. Most prepare students not only in acupuncture but also in other aspects of Chinese medicine. Students usually get a bachelor's degree. In some states, however, acupuncturists must be medical doctors; in other states chiropractors can practice acupuncture. Certification and licensing requirements also vary from state to state. Usually, after meeting the educational requirements, graduates take an examination offered by the National Certification Commission for Acupuncture and Oriental Medicine.

Chiropractors

Chiropractors believe that all body systems are related. What happens to one body part affects all the others. Chiropractors use spinal adjustments or manipulation, massage, acupuncture, and physiotherapy. Physiotherapy includes exercise, water, heat, cold, electrical stimulation, ultrasound, and traction. Chiropractors also teach their patients about good nutrition, the importance of exercise and getting enough sleep, and how to make other health-promoting lifestyle changes. They do not prescribe medication or perform surgery.

In sports medicine practices, chiropractors take medical histories, perform physical exams, order X rays, and make treatment plans with patients. Together, they make plans for short-term and long-term treatment. When indicated, chiropractors refer patients to medical specialists. Chiropractors may work in a solo practice, with a group of other chiropractors, or in a health-care facility. Some act as consultants to sports teams or specialize in sports medicine. They need to be good listeners and communicators. Observational skills are very important, and manual dexterity is a must.

If you are a high school student interested in a career as a sports medicine chiropractor, you should take the usual science classes recommended for sports medicine professionals, as well as English and another language. Computer and business courses will be especially important for those who end up in a private practice. Some young people get the idea of becoming a chiropractor because their parents have gone to chiropractors. You may be able to set up a "shadowing" or volunteer experience in a chiropractor's office. Some chiropractic colleges also offer shadowing experiences.

Chiropractic programs usually prefer students who have a bachelor of science degree. In the first two years of chiropractic college, classroom work includes courses in anatomy and physiology, biochemistry, nutrition, microbiology, and pathology. The second two years emphasize clinical skills; students work with patients under close supervision. At graduation, students receive the Doctor of Chiropractic degree.

Chiropractors must get licensed in the states in which they want to work. The most common way to get licensed is to pass the test given by the National Board of Chiropractic Examiners. To maintain their licenses, chiropractors need to get continuing education credits.

Sports Massage Therapists

Anyone who has ever had a massage after a grueling game or workout can recognize the importance of massage therapists in sports medicine. Massage therapists use their hands to relax muscles, stimulate circulation, and relieve stress, anxiety, and pain. Although massage is an ancient art, it has expanded in scope and acceptance in the last twenty years.

Currently, massage therapies are divided into several different categories, but most of the massage practiced in the United States comes from the Western form. This type of massage, which includes kneading, gliding, and friction techniques, is called Swedish because of the Swedish physician who developed it. Swedish massage is a massage of the entire body. The massage therapist uses sweeping strokes to reduce tension and promote relaxation.

Sports massage may focus on a particular muscle group or on the whole body. Athletes often have regular sessions of massage, called maintenance therapy, to keep muscles relaxed and to keep the athlete relaxed. At other times an athlete comes in immediately before a game for a warm-up massage, or after a game for a post-event massage.

Massage therapists work in quiet, relaxing spaces. Sometimes they have calming music in the background. Sports massage therapists may have private practices in their homes, or they may go to a client's home. They may have a contract with a health and fitness club and use the club facilities for their massages. Massage therapists often cooperate with other professionals, such as physical therapists, chiropractors, athletic trainers, and coaches.

Practicing massage therapy is hard physical work and may also make emotional demands on the therapist. Sometimes clients confide in massage therapists as if they are psychological counselors. If you are considering a career in massage therapy, be ready to care about the whole person as well as about his or her muscles.

You will want to take relevant courses in high school, such as anatomy, biology, speech, and communication. If you plan to be self-employed, you will need to know something about running a small business and how to market yourself. Physical education classes will not only help you keep physically fit but will help you to understand how athletes' muscles feel.

Although regulations concerning the education of massage therapists vary from state to state, most people will want to attend a school of massage therapy accredited by the American Massage Therapy Association. Accredited programs offer students training in cardiopulmonary resuscitation (CPR) and first aid, and classes in kinesiology, anatomy and physiology, the theory and practice of massage therapy, ethics, and business practices. The bulk of the instruction consists of classroom and actual practice in massage therapy. Most schools require at least 500 hours of instruction.

Certification and licensing regulations also vary among states. In 1992, a national certification system was established. The National Certification Board for Therapeutic Massage and Bodywork administers the program. The American Massage Therapy Association offers a certification in sports massage. Before getting a job, it's a good idea to serve an internship or perform volunteer work with a certified massage therapist.

Other Related Careers

There are hundreds of careers in holistic massage and bodywork. How can you tell which one might be right for you? The best way would be to try some of them. Maybe you will become interested in a particular approach and maybe not. *Nexus,* a holistic journal, suggests several questions you might ask. What is the general approach and philosophy? What credentials are offered? How does this particular kind of bodywork apply to your problems or interests? Is the approach symptomatic or holistic?

The following is a partial list of bodywork approaches: Aikido and Ki Aikido, Alchemical Bodywork, Alexander Technique, AMMA Therapy, Aston Patterning, Bioenergetics and Core Energetics, Body-Mind Insight Therapy, Bowen Technique, Breema Bodywork, Chi Nei Tsan, Core Bodywork, Cranial Osteopathy/Cranio-Sacral Therapy, Dance Therapy, Deep Tissue Bodywork, Feldenkrais, Haelan Work, Hakomi, Hellerwork, HEMME Approach, Hoshino Therapy, Integrative Massage, Jin Shin Jitsu, LooyenWork, Myofascial Release, Myotherapy, Neuro-Muscular Therapy, Ortho-Bionomy, Pfrimmer Deep Muscle Therapy, Point Holding, Polarity Therapy, Posteral Integration, Qigong, Rebalancing, Reflexology, Reiki, Rolfing, Rosen Method, Rubenfeld Synergy Method, Shiatsu, Soma Neuromuscular Integration, Tai Chi Chuan (Tai Chi), Therapeutic Touch, Touch for Health, Trager, Watsu (Water Shiatsu), Yoga, Zen Shiatsu, and Zero Balancing.

For further information about bodywork careers, you can contact the International Association of Healthcare Practitioners at (800) 233-5880 or http://www.iahp.com.

Sports Medicine Paraprofessional Careers

6

Sports medicine offers careers to those who, for one reason or another, do not want to face more years of formal education after high school. If you are interested in any of these careers, make contact with other sports medicine professionals. Chances are that you won't get to spend all of your hours performing sports medicine, but you will get to do some general work in your chosen career. The technicians mentioned in this chapter work under the supervision of other sports medicine professionals. Many of them believe that the best thing that has happened to them in their chosen careers is having a nurturing supervisor.

Biomedical Equipment Technicians

An orthopedic surgeon sends Dan, who has had arthroscopic surgery the day before, home with a passive motion machine to keep his joint moving. What if this machine suddenly stops? If this piece of electronic equipment stops functioning, Dan's rapid recovery may also stop. Who fixes the machine? The sports biomedical equipment technician, of course.

In our increasingly electronic world, biomedical equipment technicians are in demand. They repair and keep in working order the thousands of machines used in diagnosing and treating patients, medically and surgically. Those interested in becoming sports biomedical equipment technicians will probably be able to carve out a niche for themselves in this growing field.

Not only do biomedical equipment technicians fix equipment, they have to perform preventive maintenance to keep the machines from breaking down in the middle of an important medical or surgical procedure. Technicians also install new pieces of equipment and train other health-care workers in their use. Technicians may perform relatively simple repairs in a hospital or clinic, or they may work at outside shops. A technician may travel from one clinic or hospital to another. However, biomedical equipment technicians do not spend all of their time with machines. They often interact with other health-care professionals and their patients.

Because of the need to teach others, those interested in a career as a biomedical equipment technician should work on their communication skills, as well as their electronic skills. Attention to detail is a must. Courses to take in high school include science, math, computer science, and shop classes. The degree that might be most useful for a person interested in a career as a biomedical equipment technician is an associate's degree in medical electronics technology. Other possible programs that you could explore at a community college are biomedical instrument technology or electronic engineering technology. If an internship is offered, take it. Or do volunteer work in a hospital or clinic.

Although certification is not required for a job as a biomedical equipment technician, a certificate is likely to be meaningful to prospective employers. The Association for the Advancement of Medical Instrumentation certifies candidates who pass a written test.

Dental Assistants and Dental Laboratory Technicians

Dental assistants have a range of possible duties that may be applicable to sports medicine. The varied nature of this career makes it interesting. Dental assistants take care of dental equipment. For example, they sterilize equipment and prepare instrument trays. They assist the dentist with procedures, take and process X rays, prepare materials for dental restorations and impressions, teach patients about good oral hygiene, and try to put anxious patients at ease. Some dental assistants work in the clerical and business part of the office. They answer telephones, schedule and bill patients, maintain patient records, order supplies, and oversee office personnel. Since no one person can do all of the above tasks, especially in a large office, the categories may be divided into "chairside" (directly assisting the dentist) and administrative activities.

The duties of a dental assistant may depend on the regulations of a particular state. Extended Functional Dental Assistants (EFDAs) or Extended Duty Dental Assistants (EDDAs), titles accepted in some states, can take on extra responsibilities because they have had additional training.

Dental assistants usually work in clean, quiet, and well-lighted dental offices. The office may have one dentist or several. In a large office, the dental assistant may also work with dental hygienists, other dental assistants, and even dental technicians. If the dentist acts as a consultant to a sports team, a number of athletes may come in as patients. One problem that often brings athletes into a dental office is missing teeth. The dental assistant may help the dentist in performing an implant, which is a small post anchored to the jaw. The dentist can then attach an artificial tooth to the post.

If you are interested in becoming a dental assistant, you should have a calm manner with patients, especially those who are terrified of dentists. You also need a gentle touch and must be able to pay close attention to details. Plan to graduate from high school, and while you're there take as many science, business, and computer classes as you can.

Rosemary Montez is a dental assistant. In spite of pressure from her parents and high school counselors, she did not want to go to college. The year after her graduation from high school, she went on an exchange program to Mexico where she became fluent in Spanish. When she returned to the states, she considered a career as an EMT (emergency medical technician) but decided she wasn't the type to work well in a crisis. She prefers to work in a quiet office, even though she's on her feet a lot. "I like the people who come in," she says. "Also, I have steady work with good medical benefits and free dentistry for me and my daughter."

Graduation from an accredited school will make employers more interested in hiring you. Most dental assistants either attend a two-year community college program, which leads to an associate's degree, or they attend a one-year program at a technical or vocational school, where they receive a diploma or a certificate. Some states require dental assistants to get licensed or registered; others do not.

The American Dental Assistants Association is the professional organization of dental assistants; the American Dental Association's Commission on Dental Accreditation sets standards for dental assistant programs. An assistant who has only had on-the-job training or who has graduated from a nonaccredited school can take the certifying exam after two years as a full-time dental assistant.

Dental technicians work with dentists to make prosthetic dental devices. The athlete who is missing a tooth—or several teeth—will get his bridge, implant, and dentures from a dental tech. First the dentist writes a prescription for the needed dental device and then sends an impression of the patient's mouth to the dental technician, who creates a plastic model of the mouth. The technician examines the model and shapes a wax tooth using small instruments called wax spatulas and carvers. After the formation of the wax tooth, the technician pours the casts and forms the metal framework. The dental technician applies porcelain in layers over the metal. Metal bonds with porcelain, which is layered and baked until this false tooth looks like a real one. Dental technicians describe the forming of a prosthetic tooth and shading or coloring it as a work of art.

In order to do this work, which may take several days, the dental technician needs to be a patient person as well as an artist. The ability to make dental appliances is tedious work, requiring manual dexterity, mechanical ability, and good eyesight. As they do their work, dental technicians sit at a workbench, which is equipped with grinding and polishing equipment and small hand instruments.

As they gain experience, dental technicians may specialize in one of several areas, including partial dentures, full dentures, ceramics, orthodontic appliances, or crowns and bridges. Technicians can receive certification in any of these specialties. Dental technicians may have their own laboratories and be self-employed, or they may work in a commercial dental laboratory, a dentist's office, or a hospital.

If there is a chance that you're already thinking about a career as a dental technician in high school, be sure to take math, science, and business courses in addition to shop and art classes (especially ceramics), mechanical drawing, and metallurgy. In the past, most dental technicians got their only training on the job. Today, technicians can also get training at vocational-technical schools or community colleges. The college courses usually take two years and lead to an associate's degree.

Although certification is not a requirement for dental laboratory technicians, it is always a plus when applying for jobs. You will either have to have an associate's degree and two years' experience or five years' experience to take the certification exam administered by the National Association of Dental Laboratories. As a certified dental technician, you can put the initials CDT after your name. To maintain your certification, you will have to take continuing education classes.

Licensed Practical Nurses

If you have ever been a patient in a hospital or inside a doctor's office, an LPN is probably the person with whom you've had the most contact. The stated duties of LPNs vary from state to state but generally involve direct patient care.

Licensed practical nurses usually work under the supervision of a registered nurse (RN). In a sports medicine setting, LPNs may assist before or after surgery. They take vital signs (temperature, pulse, and respiration). They help prepare patients for examinations, tests, and surgery. They make sure patients are comfortable and have what they need, physically and emotionally. In most states they can administer medications. They observe patients and report symptoms and changes in a patient's condition to an RN or doctor.

Perhaps the most important quality for anyone considering a career as a licensed practical nurse is empathy. Are you a caring person? Empathy and caring are qualities that cannot be taught; you either have them or you don't. The ability to care about people, especially those in pain, without getting too emotionally involved is a gift. Do you think you could listen to patients, anticipate their needs, and communicate them to others? In addition, LPNs are often on their feet for entire shifts; good physical health and stamina are important.

Some people report that they've thought of nursing as a career for as long as they can remember. If this describes you, and you don't want to be in school for too long, consider becoming a licensed practical nurse. This career is an excellent starting place for other health-care careers and specialties such as sports medicine. In high school, don't neglect the sciences. Take as many science courses as you can, including biology and chemistry. Also be sure to work on your communication skills, both spoken and written.

You will find most LPN programs in technical and vocational schools or in community colleges. The latter leads to an associate's degree. Plan to study a range of subjects, including anatomy and physiology. Classroom teaching and clinical rotations will include a study of the various hospital departments, such as pediatrics, obstetrics and gynecology, psychiatry, and medical-surgical. Your clinical rotations will take place in hospitals or outpatient clinics. One of these clinics could be a sports medicine clinic. All fifty states and the District of Columbia require that LPNs (called LVNs in some states) be licensed.

Medical Assistants

Like dental assistants, medical assistants can do mostly clerical or clinical tasks, or they may do some of each. People sometimes get medical assistants (MAs) confused with physician assistants (PAs), but they are different. (Physician assistants are discussed in chapter 4.) Like physician assistants, medical assistants work under the supervision of a doctor, but the training of a medical assistant is not as long and the duties are different.

If medical assistants work in an office in which their jobs are mostly clerical, they may answer the telephone, schedule appointments, perform typing and medical transcription duties, act as intermediaries with insurance companies, bill patients, perform bookkeeping payroll functions, and follow up on test results. If medical assistants have mostly clinical responsibilities, they may take patients' weights, heights, temperatures, and blood pressures. They may also take medical histories, make patients comfortable, prepare patients for examinations and procedures, assist with routine tests, give medications and injections, and draw blood.

If they work in a certain kind of office or clinic, medical assistants may specialize. The assistants who work in a sports medicine clinic or in the office of an orthopedic surgeon, podiatrist, or chiropractor might consider themselves sports medicine specialists. Because of the variety, the work of a medical assistant is unlikely to be routine or boring, but it can get hectic. The assistant's schedule is tied to the doctor's schedule.

If you think you would like to become a medical assistant, ask yourself these questions: Do I genuinely care about people and like working with them? Am I a good listener and communicator? Do I enjoy performing some business and clerical jobs? Do I enjoy taking directions and working with other staff? Do I have plenty of energy and willingness to learn new skills? High school subjects that will be useful are science, math, health, business, and computers.

To get an education as a medical assistant, you can go to a community or junior college for two years and get an associate's degree. Courses are likely to include anatomy and physiology, first aid and CPR, medical terminology, principles of pharmacology, business courses (such as accounting, record keeping, and insurance processing), and office practices. The other approach to education as a medical assistant is through a year-long vocational school program. Some type of internship or clinical rotation will also be a part of your program. Before you register for a medical assistant program, try to get a shadowing experience in a clinic or in an office. Volunteering in a sports medicine clinic would be another good idea.

Medical assistants can get certified in two different ways. If you get certified by the American Association of Medical Assistants, you will get the initials CMA after your name. If you get certified by the American Medical Technologists, you will be a registered medical assistant, or RMA.

Physical Therapy Assistants

Physical therapy assistants work under the supervision of a physical therapist to help patients regain mobility. A sports physical therapist works with athletes—from the weekend type to the professional—in a sports medicine clinic or sports facility.

The physical therapy assistant is usually part of a team that includes a physician and a physical therapist, and sometimes health professionals from other disciplines. After the initial evaluation and the formulation of a treatment plan, the PT assistant will help the patient with the desired therapy, make observations, and keep accurate records. Because each patient has an individualized plan, the work of the PT assistant is rarely boring. Teaching patients how to use adaptive devices, such as crutches and braces, is another of the assistant's jobs. Physical therapy assistants sometimes supervise active exercises, such as the use of weights, or passive exercise, in which a machine or the therapist moves the patient's joints. Some assistants also help with clerical duties in an office or clinic.

A physical therapy assistant has to like people and be able to motivate them. A good sense of humor is important, too, because exercises may be difficult and painful and a patient is unlikely to respond to nagging. Humor works better. A physical therapy assistant should be upbeat, strong, efficient, and have good observational and communication skills.

High school students interested in a career as a sports physical therapist assistant should take the usual math, science, health, computer, and communication classes that will help any sports medicine professional or paraprofessional. Before being admitted to a physical therapy assistant school, you may have to document that you have done volunteer work in a physical therapy clinic.

Classes in a physical therapy assistant program will include anatomy and physiology, biology, psychology, and human growth and development. Students will study kinesiology and applied biomechanics, as well as the use of such treatments as heat, cold, ultrasound, electricity, water, and massage. A clinical rotation or internship will be part of the educational program. High school graduates will need to attend an accredited program, usually offered at a community college or junior college. There may be a waiting list for these popular programs, which give students an associate's degree at the end of the two-year course. Although not all states require it, most graduates will want to take the written examination leading to licensing as a physical therapy assistant.

Orthotic and Prosthetic Technicians

Orthotic and prosthetic technicians make braces, supports, and artificial limbs under the direction of orthotists or prosthetists. Orthotic and prosthetic technicians work from a prescription made by a physician for the device they construct.

Orthotic technicians shape metal and plastic into a brace or support, which they cover with layers of comfortable materials, such as felt, leather, or rubber. Prosthetic technicians make their devices out of plastic, metal, wood, or cloth. They pad and cover the prosthesis with leather, fiberglass, and plastic. Both types of technicians may use hammers, saws, drills, welding equipment, and fastening materials. Both work in laboratories or shops in hospitals, clinics, and private facilities. Orthotic and prosthetic technicians may also make cast models for proper fitting of the needed device. Technicians test devices for proper fit and make adjustments or repairs as necessary.

One of the main qualities needed for a person entering either of these fields is patience. Sometimes the appliance doesn't fit, in which case it's back to the drawing board. Sometimes patients are frustrated by the underlying condition that has caused them to need the device and are not eager to wear it. They may take out this frustration on the technician. Other important qualities for the orthotic or prosthetic technician are the ability to follow directions and written plans, and to ask questions when necessary. Technicians should be able to concentrate in a hot, noisy, or dusty workshop and still be able to turn out a quality product. Technicians should have skill in working with their hands and have good eye-hand coordination.

Not everyone goes straight from high school into a career as an orthotic or prosthetic technician, but some do. If you think you have what it takes in personal characteristics, be sure to take shop, classes in oral and written communication, math, sciences such as physics, and computer courses. After you get your high school diploma, you will want to get at least two years of clinical experience under the supervision of a certified orthotist, prosthetist, or orthotist-prosthetist. The other option is to enroll in a one- or two-year training program in a technical or community college, get supervised training in addition to formal courses, and graduate with an associate's degree. Because so few programs exist, most people take the former route.

Although certification is not required, it is always a plus. After completing the required education, a technician can get registered by passing a written and practical examination. The American Board for Certification in Orthotics and Prosthetics, Inc., supervises the registration program. Those wishing to specialize in sports medicine will probably have to generalize at first.

Surgical Technician

Because the orthopedic surgeon is often the hub of the sports medicine clinic, it is not surprising to find the sports surgical technician on the team. Today's surgeons perform many kinds of sports surgery on an outpatient basis (same-day surgery). Even though arthroscopy is performed through a scope, it is still surgery.

71

Surgical technicians begin their work in the pre-operative period and finish it in the postoperative period. In between, they assist with the operation. Keeping everything sterile to prevent infection is one of the surgical technician's main responsibilities. Surgical technicians make sure that the equipment to be used is sterile and that the area (the surgical field) in which the surgery will take place is also sterile. In addition to getting scrubbed, the technician may help the surgeon and nurses with their gowns and gloves. During surgery, technicians assist surgeons by giving them needed supplies, such as needles, sutures, sponges, and surgical instruments.

After the operation, the surgical technician counts everything that was used to make sure nothing was left inside the patient, sees to the disposition of specimens, and may help with the application of dressings. Technicians oversee the transportation of patients to the recovery room or hospital unit, and then clean up the operating room.

If you think you might like a career as a surgical technician, be sure that you won't faint at the sight of blood. Other desirable qualities include being able to concentrate well, respond quickly in emergencies, and take orders in a sometimes tense atmosphere. You should also be able to spend lots of time on your feet. You will be ahead of the game if you take plenty of science classes in high school, such as anatomy and physiology.

Training programs, mainly in community colleges and technical schools, last anywhere from nine months to two years. From the two-year program, you will get an associate's degree; a one-year program will give you a diploma or certificate. Classes in the sciences (anatomy, physiology, microbiology, and pharmacology) will be a big part of your program. You will also learn medical terms; how to take care of patients before, during, and after surgery; and sterilization procedures. Although certification is not mandatory, it is a good credential to have. National certification will allow you to work in any state.

Getting Started in Sports Medicine

7

Deciding on a career is an awesome job. If it's any consolation, very few people go immediately to a specialty in sports medicine. But the skills and information they pick up on their way to their ultimate career are never wasted. For example, if you become a physical therapy assistant, you may eventually decide to get the extra education required to become a physical therapist. Perhaps you will start out in a general physical therapy office and later move to a specialty in sports medicine. All of the skills you've learned along the way will be useful.

Your start on a career in sports medicine may begin in high school or even earlier. Many of those who specialize in sports medicine report that early interest in athletics paved the way for their ultimate career choices. If you get overwhelmed by all that you have to do in choosing a career, get help from a professional.

Assess Your Interests

Before you jump into an educational program or even into an apprenticeship or volunteer job in sports medicine, assess your interests. Ask yourself questions like these:

- Do I enjoy working with people? Almost all careers in sports medicine involve contact with people, including working with patients and their families and with other health professionals.
- Do I enjoy studying sciences, especially those involving the human body, such as anatomy and physiology?
- Do I find myself reading articles in magazines about nutrition, sports, exercise, fitness, and health and wellness?
- Do I like participating in sports, working out, and being physically active? Active participation is not a requirement for a career in sports medicine, but it helps.
- Can I see myself working in a hospital, a sports medicine clinic, a gym, a fitness center, or on an athletic field on a daily basis?

Assess Your Learning Style and Capacity

A big consideration in deciding which career in sports medicine you might want to pursue is how much time and energy you want to invest in education and training. As you've probably noticed by now, some people have gotten jobs in sports medicine with only on-the-job training. Other careers, such as dental assistant, require at least nine months or a year of school. Some sports medicine careers, such as physical therapy assistant, require two years of school or an associate's degree. Still others, such as biomedical engineer, require a bachelor's degree with four years of college. And some sports medicine careers, such as orthopedic surgeons who specialize in sports medicine, may take four years of medical school plus at least four more years of residency and maybe even a year or two of a specialized fellowship.

In general, though not always, careers with the most education and training pay the most. Some people will fulfill the minimum requirements for a particular career and then land a super job, sometimes through a personal contact. Usually, the minimum amount of training will not be sufficient in today's competitive job market. You will need to do volunteer work and find internships to add to your academic credentials. You will benefit from a combination of education and experience. When looking into the right type of program for the career you want, ask yourself these questions:

- What training do most people get?
- Are there several options for education and training, and if so, which would work for me?
- Is the program I'm considering accredited?
- Will the program prepare me adequately for registration, licensing, or certification in my chosen field?

- Does this program have an internship?
- What additional requirements, such as continuing education, are required in this career?
- What student services are available? After graduation, is there help with job placement?

Assess Your Programs

Before you choose your career path in sports medicine, you can and should do a lot of preliminary fact-finding. Check with your school district to see if it offers any health career apprenticeships. Through such hands-on programs, you can get experience and a certificate at the end that you can show to a prospective employer. If possible, attend college open houses or orientations, talk to current and former students about their programs, or audit a class or two. Stop in at your local college or trade or technical school, and inquire about local adult education programs. You can even check out distance learning, such as correspondence courses, but you are unlikely to get your full educational requirements taken care of in this way. Collect catalogs and find out:

- What programs and courses does this educational institution offer?
- What are the requirements for admission?
- What are the costs?
- What kinds of financial aid can I receive?
- What diplomas, certificates, or degrees are awarded?
- What is the placement rate of graduates from this program?

Assess Your Finances

Do you want a career in sports medicine that will give you a quick payback for your investment? Or are you able to postpone financial rewards in pursuit of your goal? Will your parents pay for your education, or will you have to work while going to school and pay for your own education yourself? Do you want to apply for financial aid?

If your answer to the last question is yes, the best place to start to find information about financial aid is likely to be either a high school guidance counselor or a college financial aid office. There are many different types of financial aid available, including loans, grants, scholarships, fellowships, and work-study programs. Information about financial aid is available from colleges, your state, local banks, the federal government, and the military. One resource on financial aid and many other career-related matters is the *Occupational Outlook Handbook*. It is compiled and updated annually by the United States Department of Labor, and it is available at libraries and bookstores.

Make Contacts

Making personal contacts may be the most important step in getting started in a career in sports medicine, but it is often the most neglected step. "I'm too shy," "I don't have time," and "I don't know anyone in sports medicine" are frequently heard excuses.

Before Steve went to engineering school, his dad urged him to talk to a family friend, a chemical engineer.

Steve never did get around to calling the friend. After his first semester of college, he changed his major. "I just don't have an engineer's mind," said Steve. Although his dad was tempted to say, "I told you so," he managed to keep his mouth shut. Steve eventually arranged a visit to a sports medicine clinic, which he thinks got him started on a career in sports cardiology.

Friends of the family, or people your teachers may recommend, are usually happy to discuss their careers or to provide visits or shadowing experiences. People love to tell how they got started in their careers, the mistakes they made, and the joys and drawbacks of their professions.

Go to your school guidance counselor. A guidance counselor may be able to administer aptitude tests, talk with you about various sports medicine careers, help you evaluate your strengths and weaknesses, and give you an idea of appropriate technical schools, community colleges, and universities. If you have the money, you might decide to hire a private career counselor. But be careful: you'll be using money you could be saving for college. Make sure that the person has a good reputation. Get recommendations from friends or try the Web site of the National Board of Certified Counselors at http://www.nbcc.org.

Another contact is your local public librarian, school librarian, or media center specialist. A good librarian can help you cut through the maze of information available. Occupational information is available in books, sports medicine periodicals, and occupational videos.

Of course you can go on the Internet, which is available anytime. Type in your prospective career in a search engine and watch the information pop up. You'll find links to admission requirements, available courses, financial aid, career journals, professional organizations, government documents, and job openings. The United States Department of Labor and America's Job Bank list approximately a million job openings; you can access this Web site at http://www.ajb.dni.us. Other Internet resources applicable to sports medicine are listed in the back of this book.

Introduce Yourself!

If you have the chance in your freshman year of college, sign up for a survey course in sports medicine or exercise science. Courses such as these will give you information about the field of sports medicine and may also provide you with shadowing and volunteering opportunities.

Volunteering

Volunteering, sometimes called service learning, is appropriate for any field of sports medicine. Although some high schools make volunteering for forty to fifty hours a requirement for graduation, others do not. Nevertheless, volunteering is a great idea for two reasons: you can find out from the "inside" something about your field of interest, and you can develop specialized skills that colleges and universities will value. It's entirely possible that after watching other people in their jobs, you will either be more sure of your decision or you will want to switch your career focus.

Internships

An internship is a period, usually a year, of client-centered practice under the supervision of qualified professionals. If an internship is not required in your area of study, ask for one or try to set one up for yourself. Internships are valuable for several reasons. First, you will get actual, on-the-job experience in your chosen career. As with volunteering, sometimes people find out during their internship that it is not the career for them. Second, you will make valuable contacts that may lead to a job. For example, as part of her clinical practice in nursing, Donna was placed in a sports medicine clinic. Her supervisor, a woman not much older than Donna, was pregnant and wanted to cut back on her hours. She suggested to the boss that, as soon as Donna graduated, she be hired and allowed to take some of her supervisor's hours. Donna was thrilled. Without even looking for it, she had landed her first job.

Apprenticeships

Apprenticeships are formal arrangements in which one person works for another person for a certain period of time in return for instruction in a trade, art, or business. Sports medicine is not a common field for apprenticeships. Still, you might want to look into the possibility of an apprenticeship. Sometimes apprenticeships are combined with formal learning experiences. Getting an apprenticeship may be as difficult as getting a job but may in fact lead to a job.

Getting That First Job

Now that you have your education, how do you get a job? One of your most important resources will be people. Sometimes you will have to make a supreme effort to meet those who can help you; they won't be lining up outside your door. As former athletic trainer Tom Healian said earlier in the book, every job he ever got in his thirty-two-year career came from an earlier personal contact. As he followed up on leads, one personal contact led to another.

When you're getting started, no job should be too small. You have to start somewhere. Never slack off or do a sloppy job; people will remember that. On the other hand, if you always give 100 percent, people will remember that, too. Don't forget to talk to relatives, friends, and neighbors. Make lists of the people you've contacted and those you still need to contact. Current and former employees of a health club or sports medicine clinic can tell you what it's like to work there. If you let them know you're interested, they may be willing to let you know about upcoming job openings in your specialty.

It won't hurt while you're still in high school or college to start reading the classifieds in newspapers and professional journals. When you graduate, you'll have a good idea about what employers are looking for. And don't forget the Internet. Use search keywords, like "athletic trainers," to zero in on the job listings posted by field or discipline.

Don't forget the telephone book. The yellow pages can give you ideas of places to contact. Look under your area of specialization—for example, "Rehabilitation," "Nurses," "Health, Fitness and Nutrition Consultants,"

"Hospitals," or "Sports Training and Conditioning." The career center at your college may have information on various sports medicine employers. Also, there is nothing wrong with going into sports medicine facilities and asking if they are hiring or if you can leave your résumé.

The United States Department of Labor offers two publications that should be helpful in getting that first job. *Tips for Finding the Right Job* gives suggestions on determining your job skills, organizing your job search, writing a résumé, and doing your best in a job interview. *Job Search Guide: Strategies for Professionals* discusses steps people can use to find employment. Included are sections on assessing your personal interests and skills, organizing your resources, researching the job market, and conducting a job search. You can order these publications from the U.S. Government Printing Office at (202) 512-1800, or though the Internet at http://www.gpo.gov or http://www.dol.gov.

You can get additional free help from position papers published by the National Association for Sport and Physical Education, 1900 Association Drive, Reston, VA, 20191, and the National Collegiate Athletic Association, 6201 College Boulevard, Overland Park, KS, 66211.

Sports Medicine Careers

acupuncturists Sports acupuncturists are trained in the ancient Chinese method of using fine needles inserted into certain places of the skin, with the goal of reducing pain and improving body functioning.

aerobics instructors Aerobics instructors lead the type of exercises designed to increase oxygen uptake and improve the functioning of the heart and lungs.

athletic trainers Athletic trainers recognize, evaluate, take care of, and try to prevent athletic injuries. They also counsel and educate athletes in addition to organizing and administering athletic training programs, usually at the high school, college, or professional level.

biomedical engineers Sports biomedical engineers, also called biomechanists, investigate the effects of internal and external forces on human bodies at rest or in motion. They also use engineering concepts to invent or improve devices used to diagnose and treat sports injuries.

biomedical equipment technicians Sports biomedical equipment technicians maintain and repair machines used in the diagnosis and treatment of athletes with sports injuries.

cardiologists Sports cardiologists specialize in the treatment and prevention of diseases of the heart and blood vessels in athletes.

chiropractors Sports chiropractors use spinal adjustments and manipulation, as well as holistic techniques, to treat injured athletes.

dental assistants Sports dental assistants perform a variety of jobs, from helping the dentist "chairside" to reassuring and preparing patients and performing clerical duties like scheduling, billing, and keeping patient records.

dental laboratory technicians Sports dental laboratory technicians follow dentists' prescriptions for replacement of missing or damaged teeth. They make inlays, bridges, crowns, dentures, and braces.

dentists Sports dentists work with athletes who have injuries to their teeth. They also work on the prevention and treatment of gum diseases and tooth decay, as well as filling, pulling, and replacing teeth.

dieticians/nutritionists Sports dieticians and nutritionists work as consultants with athletic teams and individual athletes to promote healthy eating, suggest dietary modifications, provide counseling on weight gain or loss, and give information about available dietary supplements. They also deal with other dietary matters thought to affect athletic performance.

exercise physiologists Exercise physiologists help people get the most from their exercise, either one-on-one with athletes, with entire teams, or in research.

holistic physicians Sports holistic physicians are conventionally trained doctors who use some alternative therapies for athletes in their practices.

licensed practical nurses Sports licensed practical nurses work in sports medicine clinics, offices of orthopedic surgeons, and in hospitals to give basic patient care to injured athletes.

massage therapists Sports massage therapists give warm-up, maintenance, and follow-up massages to athletes.

medical assistants Sports medical assistants perform clinical or clerical jobs as prescribed by state law in sports medicine offices or hospitals.

ophthalmologists Sports ophthalmologists work with athletes who have had eye injuries.

optometrists Sports optometrists examine athletes' eyes, prescribe glasses and contact lenses, prescribe medications to treat eye conditions, and sometimes practice sports vision therapy to try and improve an athlete's performance.

orthopedic surgeons Sports orthopedic surgeons diagnose and treat athletic injuries that have caused damage to the musculoskeletal system.

orthotic and prosthetic technicians Sports orthotic and prosthetic technicians work with the sports orthotist and prosthetist to design, make, fit, and maintain orthotic and prosthetic devices.

orthotist Sports orthotists design, make, and fit braces and other supports for athletes who have weakened or injured body parts.

orthotist-prosthetist Sports orthotists-prosthetists combine two separate but related sports medicine careers. They design, make, and fit braces and other supports for athletes, and also make artificial devices for those athletes who have lost a limb or part of a limb.

osteopaths Sports osteopaths sometimes use accepted medical and surgical treatments but may also use physical manipulation and other hands-on techniques to treat the whole athlete.

personal trainers Personal trainers work one-on-one with an athlete to evaluate that person's potential, design a personalized athletic training program, and demonstrate and oversee the use of equipment while offering encouragement.

physiatrists Because sports physiatrists specialize in physical medicine and rehabilitation, they are often called rehab doctors. They are trained to evaluate and treat diseases of the nerves and muscles, including sports injuries.

physical therapists Sports physical therapists work with athletes to relieve pain and help them regain mobility after injuries and surgery.

physical therapy assistants Sports physical therapy assistants prepare athletes physically and mentally for physical therapy procedures; they also help with these procedures.

podiatrists Sports podiatrists diagnose and treat diseases and injuries of the feet and lower legs.

prosthetists Sports prosthetists design, make, and fit artificial limbs for athletes.

psychologists Sports psychologists observe, describe, and explain the various mental and emotional factors that affect athletes. They also help athletes acquire the needed psychological skills to compete to the best of their abilities.

registered nurses Sports registered nurses assist physicians who work in sports medicine clinics, orthopedic clinics, or hospitals in caring for athletes who have had athletic injuries.

sports medicine physicians Sports medicine physicians work with athletes in the treatment and prevention of athletic injuries.

strength and conditioning coaches Strength and conditioning coaches use weights and machines to help athletes increase their ability to exert and resist force, thereby improving their athletic performances.

surgical technicians Sports surgical technicians, also called operating room technicians, assist the surgical team preoperatively and postoperatively, as well as during surgery.

team physicians Team physicians are doctors who work with or consult with athletic teams at both the professional and nonprofessional levels.

Glossary

acupressure A therapeutic technique that uses pressure on designated body areas.

acupuncture A traditional Chinese method using fine needles inserted into the skin, with the goal of reducing pain or improving body functioning.

aerobic Pertaining to the use of oxygen or air.

aerobic exercise Physical exertion requiring extra effort by the heart and lungs.

anatomy The study of the structures and organs of the body.

anterior cruciate ligament A band of fibrous tissue that attaches the tibia to the femur at the knee.

anxiety A vague, uneasy, uncomfortable feeling, the cause of which is probably unknown to the person who has it.

arthroscope An instrument incorporating a light source, fiber optics, and a television camera used in the diagnosis and treatment of diseased or injured joints.

biochemistry The study of the chemical substances and processes of living matter.

biomechanics The study of mechanical laws and their application to living things.

blood pressure The pressure of the blood on artery walls.

cardiopulmonary resuscitation (CPR) Restoration of adequate breathing and pulse rate by mouth-to-mouth respiration and rhythmical chest compression.

cardiorespiratory Having to do with the cardiac and respiratory systems of the body.

cardiovascular Pertaining to the heart and blood vessels.

cerebral palsy A disorder of motor functioning caused by a nonprogressive brain defect present at birth or from an event happening shortly after birth.

certification A declaration that a person has satisfied specific requirements for acceptance into a profession or other group.

degenerative disease A condition with deterioration of structure or function.

dehydration Excessive loss of body water.

echocardiography A diagnostic procedure using ultrasonic waves that studies the structure and motion of the heart.

electrocardiography A procedure that measures the electrical activity of the heart.

empathy The ability to recognize and share other people's emotions and understand the meaning of those emotions for them.

exercise Any action that causes muscle exertion or conditions the body to improve health and maintain fitness.

fine-motor skills   The ability to use precise, coordinated movement in small activities, such as writing, stitching, cutting, and visual tracking.

gynecology   The study of diseases of the female reproductive system.

hamstrings   Any one of the three muscles at the back of the thigh.

health maintenance organization (HMO)   A kind of group health-care practice that provides health services to those who prepay a fixed periodic fee.

holistic   Pertaining to the whole person and considering all factors, including physical, emotional, psychological, and spiritual events in that person's life.

humanities   Courses such as literature, languages, and philosophy (as distinguished from science courses).

interdisciplinary   Involving two or more disciplines or fields.

internship   A learning and supervised position, usually for a year, held by a recent health-care program graduate.

kinesiology   The study of the anatomical and mechanical basis of human movement.

ligament   A band of tough, fibrous connective tissue holding bones together.

medical ethics   Moral principles that govern medical decisions.

microbiology   That part of biology concerned with the study of microorganisms; in medicine, specifically those causing disease.

muscular dystrophy   An inherited muscle disease.

musculoskeletal   Pertaining to the muscles and bones.

myoelectric technology Technology that deals with the electric properties of muscle tissue.

obstetrics The branch of medicine dealing with pregnancy and childbirth.

paraprofessionals In medicine, health-care workers trained to work under the supervision of another person, usually a doctor.

patellar tendonitis An inflammation of the tendons surrounding the kneecap.

pathology The microscopic study of the tissues involved in disease.

pediatrics The branch of medicine dealing with the development and care of children.

pharmacology The study of the uses of medications.

physiology The study of the processes and functioning of the human body or other living organism.

premed Slang for premedical education or a premed student.

psychiatry The branch of medical practice dealing with the treatment and prevention of emotional, medical, and behavioral disorders.

psychology The study of the function and processes of the mind.

range of motion The movement of the bones around a joint through the arc of a circle.

scrubbing The cleansing of a person's arms and hands in preparation for performing surgical procedures.

statistics The science that deals with the collection, analysis, and interpretation of numerical data.

stress Physical, emotional, or mental tension that can cause bodily reactions.

stroke A sudden cerebral malfunction caused by the blockage or breaking of a blood vessel.

suturing Stitching together torn edges of a wound or incision.

tai chi A Chinese martial art and form of meditative exercise with slow, circular, stretching motions.

traction The use of weights and pulleys to immobilize or stretch bones or muscles to promote healing and remove pain.

treadmill An exercise machine that allows people to walk or run in place on a continuously moving belt.

yoga A series of postures and breathing exercises designed to achieve control of the mind and body.

For More Information

Sports Medicine Periodicals

AAPA News
American Association of Physician Assistants
950 North Washington Street
Alexandria, VA 22314

*Alternative Health Practitioner: The Journal of
    Complementary and Natural Care*
Springer Publishing Company
536 Broadway
New York, NY 10012

American Academy of Physician Assistants Journal
Medical Economics Publishing Company, Inc.
Five Paragon Drive
Montvale, NJ 07645

*American Academy of Podiatric Sports
    Medicine Newsletter*
1729 Glastonberry Road
Potomac, MD 20854

American Chiropractic Association Journal
American Chiropractic Association, Inc.
1701 Clarendon Road
Arlington, VA 22209

American Chiropractor
Busch Publishing
5005 Rivera Court
Fort Wayne, IN 46825

*American College of Sports Medicine Career
    Services Bulletin*
P.O. Box 1440
Indianapolis, IN 46202

American Journal of Acupuncture
1840 41st Avenue
Suite 102
Box 610
Capitola, CA 95010

American Journal of Sports Medicine
American Orthopaedic Society for Sports Medicine
P.O. Box 830259
Birmingham, AL 35282

American Psychologist
American Psychological Association
750 First Street NE
Washington, DC 20002

ASDA News
American Student Dental Association
211 East Chicago Avenue
Chicago, IL 60611

Athletic Therapy Today
Human Kinetics Publishers, Inc.
P.O. Box 5076
Champaign, IL 61825

Clinical Journal of Sport Medicine
University of Calgary
Sports Medicine Center
2500 University Drive NW
Calgary, Alberta T2N 1N4

Clinics in Sports Medicine
Periodicals Fulfillment
W. B. Saunders Company
6277 Sea Harbor Drive, 4th Floor
Orlando, FL 32891

Health and Fitness Journal
Lippincott, Williams & Wilkins
P.O. Box 1610
Hagerstown, MD 21741

High Performance Optometry
Anadem Publishing, Inc.
3620 North High Street
Columbus, OH 43214

Imprint
National Student Nurse's Association
555 West 57th Street
New York, NY 10019

Journal of the American Dental Association
American Dental Association
211 East Chicago Avenue
Chicago, IL 60611

Journal of the American Dietetic Association
American Dietetic Association
216 West Jackson Boulevard, Suite 800
Chicago, IL 60606

Journal of Applied Biomechanics
Human Kinetics Publishers, Inc.
P.O. Box 5076
Champaign, IL 61825

Journal of Applied Sport Psychology
Centennial Conferences
4800 Baseline Road
Boulder, CO 80303

Journal of Athletic Training
National Athletic Trainers' Association
2952 North Stemmons Freeway
Dallas, TX 75247

Journal of Orthopaedic and Sports Physical Therapy
Lippincott, Williams & Wilkins
P.O. Box 1610
Hagerstown, MD 21741

Journal of Prosthetics and Orthotics
American Academy of Orthotists and Prosthetists
1650 King Street, Suite 500
Alexandria, VA 22314

Journal of Sport Psychology
Human Kinetics Publishers, Inc.
Box 5076
Champaign, IL 61825

Journal of Sport Rehabilitation
Human Kinetics Publishers, Inc.
Box 5076
Champaign, IL 61825

Journal of Strength and Conditioning Research
The Human Performance Laboratory
Ball State University
Muncie, IN 47306

Massage and Bodywork Quarterly
Associated Bodywork and Massage Professionals
1271 Sugarbush Drive
Evergreen, CO 80439

Massage Therapy Journal
American Massage Therapy Association
820 Davis Street, Number 100
Evanston, IL 60201

Medicine and Science in Sports and Exercise
Lippincott, Williams & Wilkins
P.O. Box 1610
Hagerstown, MD 21741

Nursing: The World's Largest Nursing Journal
Springhouse Corporation
111 Bethlehem Pike
Box 908
Springhouse, PA 19477

Optometry and Vision Science
Lippincott, Williams & Wilkins
P.O. Box 1610
Hagerstown, MD 21741

The Physician and Sportsmedicine
4530 West 77th Street
Minneapolis, MN 55435

PMA: Professional Medical Assistant
American Association of Medical Assistants
20 North Wacker Drive, Suite 1575
Chicago, IL 60606

Sports Medicine Digest
Lippincott, Williams & Wilkins
P.O. Box 1610
Hagerstown, MD 21741

Surgical Technologist
Association of Surgical Technologists, Inc.
7108-C South Alton Way
Englewood, CO 80112

Web Sites

Aerobics and Fitness Association of America
http://www.afaa.com

American Academy of Ophthalmology
http://www.aao.org

American Academy of Orthopaedic Surgeons
http://www.aaos.org

American Academy of Orthotists and Prosthetists
http://www.oandp.com/academy

American Academy of Physician Assistants
http://www.aapa.org

American Alliance for Health, Physical Education,
    Recreation, and Dance
http://www.aahperd.org

American Association of Medical Assistants
http://www.aama-ntl.org

American Association of Oriental Medicine
http://www.aaom.org

American Chiropractic Association
http://www.amerchiro.org

American College of Sports Medicine
http://www.acsm.org

American Dental Assistants Association
http://www.dentalassistant.org

American Dental Association
http://www.ada.org

American Dietetic Association
http://www.eatright.org

American Health Care Association
http://www.ahca.org

American Holistic Health Association
http://www.ahha.org

American Holistic Medical Association
http://www.holisticmedicine.org

American Massage Therapy Association
http://www.amtamassage.org

American Nurses Association
http://www.nursingworld.org/about

American Optometric Association
http://www.aoanet.org/aoanet

American Psychological Association
http://www.apa.org

American Society of Contemporary Medicine, Surgery,
   and Ophthalmology
http://www.ascmso.com

American Society for Nutritional Sciences
http://www.faseb.org/asns

Associated Bodywork and Massage Professionals
http://www.abmp.com

Association of American Medical Colleges
http://www.aamc.org

Association for Network Chiropractic
http://www.associationfornetworkcare.com

Association of Operating Room Nurses
http://www.aorn.org

Association of Schools and Colleges of Optometry
http://www.opted.org

Careers in Sports Medicine

Biomedical Engineering Society
http://www.mecca.org/BME/BMES/society/index.htm

International Association of Healthcare Practitioners
http://www.iahp.com

International Chiropractors Association
http://www.chiropractic.org

National Association of Dental Laboratories
http://www.nadl.org

National Association for Sport and Physical Education
http://www.aahperd.org/naspe/naspe_main.html

National Athletic Trainers' Association
http://www.nata.org

National Athletic Trainers' Association Education Council
http://www.cewl.com

National Strength and Conditioning Association
http://www.nsca-lift.org

Women's Sports Foundation
http://www.lifetimetv.com/WoSport

Worldwide Aquatic Bodywork Association
http://www.watsu.com

For Further Reading

Berger, Melvin. *Sports Medicine: Scientists at Work.* New York: Thomas Y. Crowell, 1982.

Fisher, David. *The 50 Coolest Jobs in Sports: Who's Got Them, What They Do, and How You Can Get One!* New York: Macmillan Reference USA, 1997.

Hancock, Cheryl. *Healthcare Career Starter.* New York: Learning Express, 1998.

Hayes, David, ed. *Exploring Health Careers: Real People Tell You What You Need to Know.* Chicago: Ferguson Publishing Company, 1998.

Heitzmann, William R. *Careers for Sports Nuts and Other Athletic Types.* 2nd ed. Lincolnwood, IL: VGM Career Horizons, 1997.

Heitzmann, William R. *Opportunities in Sports Medicine Careers.* Lincolnwood, IL: VGM Career Horizons, 1992.

Massengale, John D., and Richard A. Swanson, eds. *The History of Exercise and Sport Science.* Champaign, IL: Human Kinetics Publishers, Inc., 1997.

Careers in Sports Medicine

Nieman, David C. *Fitness and Sports Medicine: An Introduction.* Palo Alto, CA: Bull Publishing Company, 1990.

Simpson, Carolyn, and Penelope Hall, M.D. *Careers in Medicine.* New York: The Rosen Publishing Group, Inc., 1994.

Index

About the Author

Barbara Moe, R.N., M.S.N., M.S.W., is a nurse, social worker, and writer who likes working out. She is the author of several books, including *Coping with Mental Illness, Coping with Tourette Syndrome and Other Tic Disorders, Coping When You Are the Survivor of a Violent Crime, Coping with Eating Disorders, Coping with Bias Incidents,* and *Coping with Chronic Illness.*

Acknowledgments

I would like to acknowledge the help of Susan Armitage, R.N.; Neil Bogan; Kelly Bolig; Mike Dunn, D.D.S.; Kristen Geiger, M.D.; David Greenberg, M.D.; Michelle Haugh; Tom Healion; Charles Malek; Dan Moe; David Moe; Paul Moe, M.D.; Erin Ryan; and Charles Weaver.

Layout

Nelson Sá